THEN AND NOW

A world history of how people lived
from ancient times to the present

First published by Parragon in 2013

Parragon
Chartist House
15–17 Trim Street
Bath, BA1 1HA
www.parragon.com

This edition © Parragon Books Ltd 2013
Images © EDITORIAL SOL90 S.L.
Text © EDITORIAL SOL90 S.L.

English edition produced by
Cambridge Publishing Management Ltd

ISBN 978-1-4723-0421-6
Printed in China

THEN AND NOW

A world history of how people lived
from ancient times to the present

Parragon

Bath · New York · Singapore · Hong Kong · Cologne · Delhi
Melbourne · Amsterdam · Johannesburg · Shenzhen

CONTENTS

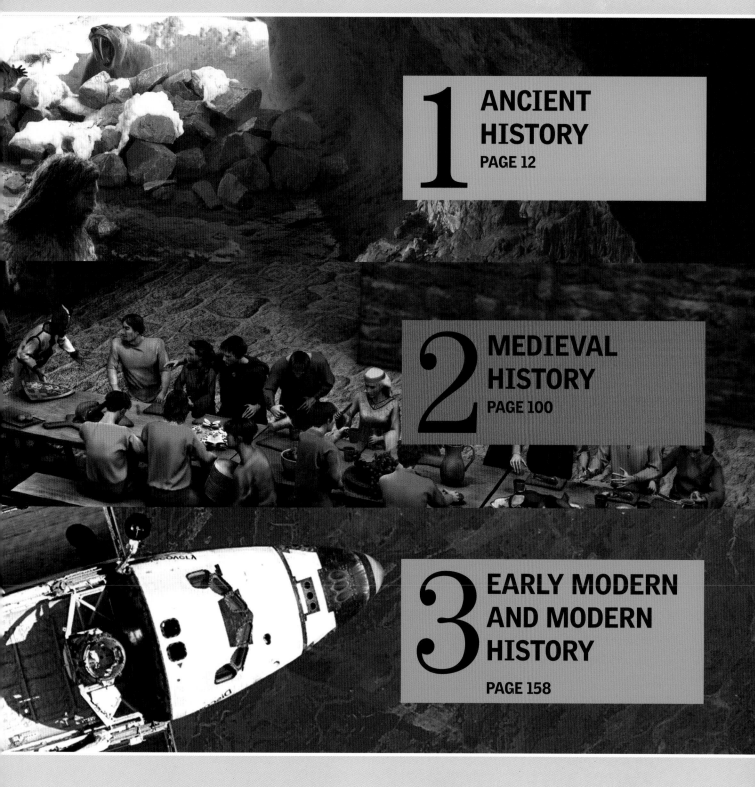

FROM ANCIENT TIMES TO THE PRESENT

The history of our world is the story of people, our ancestors, from those early humans who hunted and controlled fire, via generations of explorers who set off into the unknown, to the astronauts who freed themselves from the shackles of the planet Earth entirely. Our history is about pharaohs and queens and wealthy merchant bankers, but about slaves and nursemaids and child miners, too. *Then and Now* brings vividly to life the events witnessed and driven by humankind through the centuries.

Prehistory

From the simplest of temporary dwellings, prehistoric humankind fashioned a community in which they controlled fire, shaped tools, and hunted animals. Gradually, homes became more secure and permanent; loved ones were buried with precious possessions nearby. Rituals and ceremonies developed, and clans became more organized. They established a new relationship with the surrounding environment, and gradually became specialized at hunting, trapping prey to feed the large groups in which they lived. A dramatic transition came when humans developed agriculture, sowing crops and domesticating animals to provide readily available grain, meat, milk, and furs. Now settlements could become permanent. Indispensable knowledge was passed from generation to generation, marking the origins of inherited knowledge and education.

First Civilizations

The Neolithic period—about 4000 to 2500 BC—heralded the arrival of the first civilizations, with the trading of surplus products and the birth of commerce, practiced on a grand scale by the Phoenicians. The Sumerians of Mesopotamia built dwellings made of sun-dried mud bricks and erected imposing temples, creating urban clusters. By the end of the third millennium BC, 90 percent of Sumeria's population lived in towns or cities. The roles of men and women became more formalized: Sumerian society was dominated by men, with women confined to the domestic sphere while men controlled public areas of life.

TEACHING
Since Paleolithic times, adults have developed and passed on knowledge and skills to their children, such as how to control fire and stone-carving techniques that allowed them to develop tools and weapons.

Ancient Egypt

By contrast, women in ancient Egypt enjoyed legal autonomy—they could trade and manage their own goods, and choose their own occupations. Key to Egyptian prosperity was agriculture; the periodic Nile floods deposited rich silt that enabled people to grow a vast range of foodstuffs, such as cereals, asparagus, dates, and melons. Egyptians pursued achievements in a variety of spheres, including architecture, engineering, medicine, and astronomy, while they also developed one of the first methods of writing: hieroglyphics. The theocratic political organization had the pharaoh at its heart, who was believed to be divine. Symbolic of the society and the pharaoh's position were magnificent funerary temples, such as the Pyramid of Cheops (constructed between 2551 and 2528 BC), which even today continues to reveal treasures and secrets beyond our imaginings.

Ancient Greece

The Hellenistic period in Greece (323 BC to about the first century BC) saw powerful Greek families building comfortable and spacious dwellings. Each room had a particular use, a model for living that has continued through to the modern age. The Athenians invented the first democratic system of government; all free adult males born in Athens could participate. An education system for men spanning from infancy to adulthood culminated in the learning of disciplines necessary for participation in the political assembly, such as rhetoric, eloquence, and argument.

Ancient Rome

In Rome, the expansion of empire from the first century BC was mirrored in the city. By 50 BC, the population of Rome had reached one million. *Insulae*, or multifamily dwellings, began to be built to house growing populations. In contrast to the luxurious residences of the wealthy, these were cramped, insanitary, and prone to collapse or fires. The city was run by a closed group monopolizing all political, economic, and religious power; these "patricians" served the Roman Senate for life, producing a stable institution. By the first century AD, the Roman Empire was at its zenith, having conquered Britain and Mesopotamia in Asia by means of its ruthlessly efficient fighting legions. Its language dominated administration and communication, the latter facilitated by the extensive network of roads that united the empire.

Medieval Europe

By the Medieval period in Europe, most peasants lived in dwellings with extended families, working the land under the control of a feudal lord—the owner of the land (fiefdom) they worked and a member of the warrior nobility. From their castles and fortresses, the lords controlled every aspect of their lives.

Cities that had been heirs to the classical culture of ancient Greece and Rome entered into decline in the early Middle Ages; but from the eleventh to thirteenth centuries, Europe entered a new period of expansion and prosperity. Feudalism was consolidated, foreign invasions had ceased, land productivity increased through new technology, towns were established, and commerce expanded. A new social class—the middle class—emerged. The cities grew again, positioning themselves as the main educational centers.

Medieval Asia

A primary connection between the West and the Far East, the "Silk Road," which reached its height in the seventh and eighth centuries, was a network of routes uniting remote

GREEK THEATER
Greek theater emerged around the sixth century BC. Masks were worn, which made female characters (played by men) more realistic, and the action easier to follow when viewed in a large amphitheater.

MEDIEVAL VENICE
Medieval Venetians were supreme merchants. They traded throughout the Mediterranean, the Middle East, Central Asia, and the Far East and became enormously powerful.

China with Europe. Material goods were transported, but so were ideas, philosophical trends, religions, and inventions, from one side of the world to the other.

Islamic culture had begun to expand in the seventh century; it spread through southern and eastern Mediterranean, Eastern Europe, Asia, and Africa. Scholars excelled in subjects such as arithmetic, geometry, algebra, natural sciences, and poetry. Education occupied a central role.

Away from the cities, feudal armies—Chinese, Korean, Samurai, and Mongol—fought for supremacy. Nomadic tribes, such as the Mongols, traveled over vast areas of the Asian continent before success under their leader Genghis Khan, in the thirteenth century, allowed them to consolidate an empire comprising 100 million people over 13.5 million square miles (35 million square kilometers), challenging the centuries-old power of China. The Chinese empire had been the crucible of so many of the inventions and discoveries on which the modern world relies—including developing the compass, which allowed Christopher Columbus to reach the Americas.

Medieval America
The Aztec Empire dominated a substantial part of current Mexican territory between the fourteenth century and the Spanish conquests of the sixteenth. The Aztecs were a warrior people with a complex society and a theocratic system. As the conquistadors arrived in America, plants and animals brought over from Europe slowly adapted to their new environment and were incorporated into American diets. The Europeans brought cattle, pigs, horses, and hens; from America to Europe went corn, tomatoes, cocoa, and turkeys.

The Early Modern Period
During the fifteenth and sixteenth centuries, the cultural movement known as the Renaissance expanded through the central regions of Europe, bringing a burgeoning interest in

TRADE AND EXPLORATION
Early exploration by sea was full of danger, discomfort, and navigational difficulties. The main reason for long sea voyages was nearly always the desire to find new markets, raw materials, or trade routes.

the classical, secular culture, and scientific and geographical discovery. Elizabethan theater marked a golden age in the English Renaissance, while elsewhere in Europe, astronomers were radically changing people's view of the universe, establishing that the Earth revolved around the Sun.

Mercantile activities expanded through East and West, and from the fifteenth century numerous dynasties or family companies of merchants were formed, with headquarters and branches spread throughout Europe. They moved into industrial and banking activities, lending money to political figures and the great monarchies. The state began to intervene to control imports and exports, foster industry, seek new markets and raw materials, and fight to expand colonies and protect monopolies. The human cost of commerce was nowhere more evident than in the fate of the African slaves, traded from the sixteenth to the nineteenth centuries, who suffered great cruelty on the crop plantations of the American colonies.

The Nineteenth and Twentieth Centuries

The Industrial Revolution, which began in England around 1760, provided the initial impetus for changes in social and economic interaction. As migrants arrived in cities from rural areas to work in new factories, there was a rapid proliferation in the construction of cheap housing for working people. Meanwhile, a powerful middle class, bolstered by economic successes, became established in the major European cities. A growth in office work accompanied the development of the industrial world.

The Twentieth Century to Today

In the modern era, family structures vary widely around the world; in some regions, traditional systems of extended families, clans, and polygamy remain, whereas in the Western world the nuclear family has gained prominence. Homes take a variety of forms, while efforts have turned toward incorporating modern technologies for energy conservation and ease of use.

Urban transportation was revolutionized in the late nineteenth century with the birth of subway systems in many countries of the Western world. The modern revolution in commercial transportation has been dramatic, too, allowing for the shipment of goods over massive distances. The fishing industry has changed from a small-scale and local industry to the large-scale, transoceanic enterprise it is today, with all the threats to diversity and stocks that that implies.

The most dramatic recent change, however, has been the explosion in the use of the Internet, a development that has affected every aspect of our lives. Online divisions of known brands have been created, alongside huge "virtual" department stores, such as Amazon. Many workers can now offer services, via their computers, without leaving their homes, while major companies establish commercial relations on a worldwide scale through virtual Internet connections.

Contemplating such dramatic world events, it can seem difficult to comprehend the extraordinary changes that humankind has undergone from the earliest prehistoric societies to the present day. *Then and Now* will take you on a rollercoaster journey through time. Annotated three-dimensional reconstructions and cutaway models let you journey right into the heart of history and peer behind the scenes into the daily lives of bygone communities.

A VIRTUAL ECONOMY
The twenty-first century is characterized by a global economy, whose size, character, and way of communicating and working would have been unimaginable one hundred years ago.

1 ANCIENT HISTORY

16

4

58

78

Ancient history

Ancient history covers the period of time from the first known humans to the Roman Empire. Looking back 500,000 years reveals the very beginnings of civilization, from which we can trace the development of farming and trade, intellectual advances, such as writing, and the gradual emergence of complex social and political societies.

500,000 years ago
PREHISTORIC SHELTERS

Humankind's ancestor, *Homo erectus*, built the first dwellings of any prehistoric community. These simple temporary shelters were constructed using branches and rocks that the nomadic groups found scattered as they moved around in search of food.

5000 BC
LEARNING TO WRITE

The ancient Egyptians are known for their advances in mathematics, medicine, and astronomy. Their most important contribution to culture was the invention of one of the first methods of writing: hieroglyphics, based on images that represent ideas, beliefs, or proper names.

3200 BC
THE SUMERIANS

The Sumerians lived in Mesopotamia, in what today is Iraq. They are considered the first great civilization in history. Their most significant and lasting innovation was urbanization; at the end of the third millennium BC, 90 percent of the population of south Mesopotamia lived in cities and towns.

1350 BC
EGYPTIAN WOMEN

Nefertiti (left) was the wife and coregent of the Pharaoh Akhenaton. Thanks to her status, women from the privileged sectors started to appear in works of art beside their husbands and descendants.

900–612 BC
MEN OF IRON

The Assyrian army was composed of 200,000 men, and it used large cavalry squadrons. The Assyrians were the first to use weapons made of cast iron—far superior to those made of bronze—which gave them a key advantage over their adversaries.

776 BC
THE OLYMPIC GAMES

The first Games were held in the Olympic sanctuary in 776 BC, as part of a religious celebration in honor of Zeus. As well as sports, there were animal sacrifices and displays from sculptors and poets. Winners were considered heroes and achieved fame throughout the Greek world.

388 BC
PLATO'S ACADEMY

Plato founded this school of philosophy on the outskirts of Athens in an olive grove dedicated to the goddess Athena. "Let no one enter here who does not know mathematics" was the inscription at its entrance.

20,000 BC
HUNTING MAMMOTHS

Paleolithic man devised strategies and tools for ambushing, chasing, and cornering prey. Mammoths (right) were a favorite target: their large size ensured an abundance of meat. Even the tongue, very rich in fats, was a much-prized foodstuff.

8500–4000 BC
THE BIRTH OF TRADE

A profound consequence of humans' ability to control food production was the creation of excess. Anything surplus to need could be exchanged for other goods: different types of food, tools, and beasts of burden. Trade was born—as were social strata. Those with the most valuable items occupied the highest positions in the community.

2551–2528 BC
THE PYRAMID OF CHEOPS

Only one of the seven wonders of the ancient world has survived the passage of time: the Pyramid of Cheops in Egypt. A universal symbol of ancient Egypt, it is a colossal work of engineering, whose mysteries have still not been completely revealed.

2500 BC
LIQUID GOLD

Olives were the main crop in ancient Greece. Olive oil was also known as "liquid gold," and was used for cooking, cosmetics, and as a tribute to the gods. The oldest Greek records about olive growing come from Crete and date from approximately 2500 BC.

1750 BC
PATRIARCHY

Domestic life in ancient Mesopotamia was characterized by the authority of the man as the head of the family. Women passed from the tutelage of their father to that of their husband when they married; they had rights, but these were inferior to those of men.

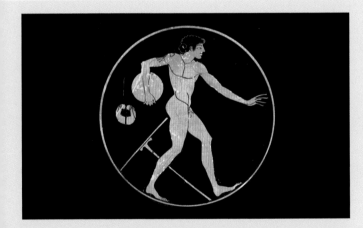

500 BC
GREEK THEATER

Theater was one of the few events where all members of a Greek family could share in a common activity. Actors, however, were single men. If a play required female characters, men covered their faces with masks and wore high-heel shoes.

264 BC
GLADIATORS

The first gladiatorial show took place in the year 264 BC. The word "gladiator" derives from *gladius*, the ancient Romans' short sword. Gladiators (left) came from the lowest social classes: they were slaves, criminals, or prisoners. However, they earned money for their work and if they were successful, they could gain their liberty.

27 BC–AD 476
ROMAN *INSULAE*

During the Roman Empire, the Romans built *insulae* to house the rapidly expanding population. These multistory constructions provided apartments for many families and were the antecedents of modern apartment buildings.

First Century AD
DRINK OF THE GODS

From antiquity, wine was used as an offering to the gods in Mediterranean cultures. The Romans adopted this tradition from their Greek neighbors, and it spread throughout Western Europe. Roman innovations in the cultivation of vines are still used in winemaking today.

AD 70–80
THE COLOSSEUM

Although there were more than 250 amphitheaters across the Roman Empire, the biggest and most famous was the Colosseum in Rome. Built in AD 70–80 by the emperor Vespasian and his son and successor Titus, it seated 50,000 spectators and provided a venue for gladiatorial contests, fights against animals, mock battles, and reenactments of mythological scenes.

Prehistory

Prehistory refers to the time before recorded history. The planet Earth is 4.5 billion years old, but humankind has inhabited it for only a fraction of that time—estimated by archaeologists to be about 200,000 years. Evolving from the *Homo erectus* that inhabited southern Africa in the Middle

Paleolithic period—some 65 million years after the event that caused the extinction of dinosaurs in the Cretaceous period— and having learned to make fire, use primitive tools, and hunt, our ancestors migrated into Eurasia and Oceania around 40,000 years ago, and reached the Americas about 14,500 years ago.

Open-Air Homes

The first dwellings built by prehistoric communities were simple temporary shelters erected in the open air. The materials used consisted of branches or rocks that the nomadic groups found scattered around as they were moving in search of food. *Homo erectus* was a hominid belonging to the order of higher primates that were the direct ancestors of humankind. To guarantee subsistence, they had to travel long distances and move quickly. By controlling fire and manufacturing sophisticated tools, they were able to adapt to differing weather conditions.

Erecting the Shelters

The dwellings of *Homo erectus* were built using branches and trunks, which were secured to the ground with heavy rocks. They were oval in shape and could be up to 50 feet (15 meters) long by 20 feet (6 meters) wide. The sturdiest trunks were positioned inside the shelter and used as posts to support the structure. There is evidence that the upper part of the branches and the more flexible pieces of wood were bent to form the roofs of these primitive huts.

SMOKE OUTSIDE
Fire was used as protection from the cold, to cook food, and to frighten away dangerous animals. The roofs had an opening to let smoke from the fires escape.

COLLABORATIVE CONSTRUCTION
The work was organized on a community basis—that is, all the members participated in the construction of the dwellings and in making the various tools.

INTELLIGENT LOCATION
The encampments were located in areas close to stretches of water. This made it easier to approach the herds that congregated near water and sustained *Homo erectus*.

DOMESTIC LIFE
The men periodically traveled away from the camps to find animal meat. This was rich in necessary proteins, although they were unaware of it. The women and children devoted their energies to gathering wild fruit and wood.

1 CAMP

Settlements consisted of one or two shelters and were suitable for twenty or so people who were related. The dwellings were collective, meaning they were made for the group in general, and they belonged to everybody, without distinction.

2 MAKING FIRE

Homo erectus was the first hominid to control fire and to make it deliberately. They picked it up from occasional forest fires and obtained it by rubbing pieces of wood together to create sparks, which they stoked up with dry straw or brushwood.

INTERNAL SPACE

The shelters, which had no internal partitions, were both single and multifunctional spaces at the same time. They were used as areas for sleeping, cooking, and making tools.

WORKED GROUND

The ground surface of the dwellings was leveled with skins or stone slabs. Fragments of tools, building materials, and remnants of food have been found scattered inside huts, such as this one.

VERY PRACTICAL TOOLS

Tools were made of stone or bone. The ax was the most revolutionary prehistoric artifact because it enabled people to cut meat and wood and also prepare hides and dig up edible roots.

In the Trees

The *Australopithecus*, considered the most ancient ancestor of human beings, used trees for shelter. They fed on fruit and leaves they found in the treetops and slept on the branches. Although they walked on two feet, they spent little time on the ground because they could not defend themselves from predators there.

Life in Caves

The use of caves as dwellings was characteristic of Western Europe, especially in what today are France and Spain. Until the end of the Paleolithic period, Neanderthal and Cro-Magnon people took maximum advantage of these natural cavities. Alternative uses for the cave were as a resting place, where they protected themselves from the cold and damp, and as a place for burial and worship. They lived in groups and shared the same space for various periods of the year. In general, they painted scenes featuring animals on their walls and ceilings. To feel safer, they built a kind of wall at the entrance. These were hard times, in which the human being struggled to survive.

Separate Spaces

Inside the cave, spaces were separated according to different activities: zones for removing hides, drying zones, areas for carving meat, and spaces for storing food. The largest area in the cave was used for sleeping. In the Upper Paleolithic period, small individual cabins were built inside the caves.

MODERN CAVES
A fire provided heat and was used to cook food. At night, this fire prevented fierce animals from entering the cave.

STONES ON THE GROUND
In the Late Paleolithic period, cave interiors were improved. To insulate the ground from humidity, it was covered with flat stones and dry leaves.

LIFE IN THE COMMUNITY
Family ties were strong. The young observed their elders to learn basic working techniques.

EVERYONE WORKED TOGETHER
Activities were distributed among the members of the group: some hunted, others manufactured tools or kept the fire burning.

The Oldest Cave

A cave in Vallonnet is the oldest cave habitat in Europe. It is located in France and was occupied 900,000 years ago. The archaeological remains reveal activities of hunting and gathering but do not show signs of working with fire.

Tent of the Paleolithic Period

With the end of the Ice Age, the ice that had covered the planet for thousands of years began to recede. These transformations meant that human beings found themselves with a new world around them. The forests and plains thriving in the temperate climate, offered better conditions for human life. People began to live in tents or semipermanent dwellings, built with mammoth bones, skins, and branches. Camps could have several of these large structures and accommodate numerous members of one or many families.

PROTECTIVE WALL
A defensive wall was usually constructed with stones or wood at the entrance. It was used to ensure that they were not caught unawares by animals, rain, or cold.

THEIR OWN WATER
On occasion, the caves had naturally formed water sources that easily provided for the whole community.

CAREFUL BURIALS
The first of our ancestors who conducted burials were the Neanderthals. The sites at which they chose to locate the bodies were far away from the entrances of the caves. First, they dug a hole and covered the bottom with small stones. Then they laid their loved one there, together with their most precious possessions, such as spears and decorations. Finally, they covered the body with earth.

CEREMONIAL SPACE
Various archaeological sites have highlighted that the deepest areas of the caves were reserved for rituals and ceremonies of a magical nature.

Group Identity

During the Mesolithic period, clans were the most widespread form of organization among humans. In general, these were large kinship groups that went beyond immediate family relations. Their members believed they descended from a common ancestor of a mythical nature, and for this reason they considered themselves a community with a distinctive identity.

Clan Ties

Mesolithic clans followed a system whereby kinship was traced either through the male or the female line. Patrilineal descendants joined the father's group automatically at birth and remained a member of this group throughout their lifetime; matrilineal descendants joined the mother's group. In patrilineal groups, males dominated; in matrilineal groups, the women were in the positions of power, controlling land and products. Clans came to be made up of hundreds of people, and membership of a clan affected every aspect of the individual's life. All the members of the group or clan were treated with the same respect and closeness as the closest family members. It was during this period that the need for exogamic unions—marriage ties between people belonging to different groups—began to spread. Strong clan relationships meant it was forbidden to join together with individuals who were members of the same clan, however far removed the kinship might have been.

Lithic Amulets

Objects such as these are anthropomorphic female figures were sculpted in stone and terra-cotta. They symbolized fertility, which was central in the cultures of transition between hunting and agriculture.

SPECIALIZATION
The increase in members required the specialization of tasks, such as, the preparation of fish and shellfish.

SURVIVAL
Scarcity meant it was necessary to forage for food every day.

1

2

Change of Habits

During the Paleolithic period, human beings depended on hunting large mammals for food. This way of life was reflected in numerous cave paintings showing hunting scenes. However, starting from the Mesolithic period, the clans established a new relationship with the natural environment and began to concern themselves with producing certain foods.

1 FISHING
Specialization with stone tools made it possible to manufacture harpoons for fishing. This task was generally reserved for men.

2 LEARNING TO DO
The diversified manual work of all the members of the clan ensured the survival of all. Working with stone, wood, and wicker was widespread.

3 FIRE UNITES
Bonfires were the meeting places of the community and the family, around which they told stories of their common ancestors.

4 BEING A MEMBER
The members of the clan considered themselves to be part of the same family. The categories of clan kinship included very long names.

The Incest Taboo

The universal practice, albeit a variable one, concerning the preference for sexual relations outside of the social group of origin is known as the incest taboo. Since the nineteenth century, various scientific theories have attempted to explain its origin and meaning.

CHALLENGING THE LAWS OF KINSHIP

The painting on this rock, which is located in the Kakadu National Park in Australia—a territory inhabited by humankind for more than twenty thousand years—represents Namondjok, the creator ancestor, who, according to local beliefs, broke the incest laws with his sister and was banished to the sky.

MEMBERSHIP
Family ties were decisive in determining the membership of the clan group.

SETTLEMENTS
They were seminomadic; they moved between alternate environments with a few belongings.

DWELLINGS
It is thought that men and women moved the tents they used for daily shelter.

THE CLAN
This concept comes from the Gaelic term *clann*—son or descendant. They were united by various kinship relations.

Hunting to Eat

In the Paleolithic period, human beings underwent a transformation from simple feeders on carrion to specializing as hunters. Progressively, they ceased to feed on dead animals and began to trap various types of prey as their main source of food. Hunting required the cooperation of all the members of a group and, for this reason, more complex forms of social organization had to be created. Mammoths were a most prized commodity because their large size ensured an abundant supply of meat, which enabled a large group of people to survive without difficulties.

Trapping Prey

Prehistoric human beings were nomadic and constantly crossed the land in search of food. Approximately one million years ago, humankind's first ancestors abandoned feeding on carrion and began to hunt to find food. Hunting required the use of special tools and also a certain level of organization among the individuals concerned in order to coordinate activities. The main prey in the Paleolithic period was medium and large animals living in herds, as is proven by the paintings found in caves. The animals hunted were generally herbivorous mammals, such as mammoths. These animals were less aggressive and slower than the carnivore species; they lived in large groups and were easier to locate, because they usually grazed near water courses. Various techniques were used for these hunting tasks: ambushing, chasing, and cornering. The hunters would usually surround a herd and, using different strategies and traps, would separate one animal from the rest of the group before killing it.

From Land to Water

Initially, people collected the crabs, small fishes, or bivalves they found exposed on the various stretches of water. They progressively incorporated tools into hunting and fishing: spears and bows and arrows.

Herds

Mammoths were a similar size to today's elephants. The herds were composed of females headed by a leader. The males lived in small groups after reaching sexual maturity.

LUCKY THROW
Spears were the main weapons used for capturing and killing mammoths.

STRATEGY
Some men produced sounds to direct the animals toward other hunters.

PREGNANT FEMALES
Humans avoided sacrificing them as a way of managing their food resources.

Menu: Megafauna

Ten thousand years ago, the large land mammals were undergoing a process of extinction, caused both by the environmental changes of the last Ice Age and by aspects of the systematic hunting of the Paleolithic period. The mammoth was one of the main animals to be hunted.

1 HUNT LEADER
The search for food was a planned activity performed by cooperating members of the group. The most able hunter was usually the leader.

2 AVAILABILITY
The natural limit on the availability of food inevitably limited the growth of the human population.

3 TOTAL CONSUMPTION
Every part of a mammoth was consumed. Even its tongue, which was very rich in fats, was a much-prized foodstuff.

4 DIVISION OF TASKS
With the exception of the leader's role, the functions of each of the hunters were usually rotated, depending on the circumstances of and requirements for each ambush.

Gathering

In prehistoric times, the population complemented its diet with the fruit and seeds that were abundant in the areas they moved in. They also learned to recognize the life cycles of plants.

MEAT
After hunting, the meat was chopped up, using hatchets, and was roasted on an open fire.

TUSKS
Humans used tusks to support the shelters and as a raw material for tools.

Gifts of the Land

The development of agriculture and livestock breeding marked a fundamental transformation in the history of humanity. For the first time, people began to settle permanently in one place and become productive groups, growing and rearing their own food. They stopped depending on what the environment gave them and began to control the production process. Gradually, a specialization of tools and a differentiation of tasks came about.

Producing Food

The first crops and domesticated animal species appeared in the Near East 10,000 years ago. Some human communities began to establish a new relationship with the natural environment: they ceased to act solely as hunters and gatherers and began to produce their own food. The first crops were cereals, due to the fact that they grow abundantly in the wild and that sowing and harvesting them is relatively easy. The earliest animals that were bred for food were goats and sheep. It is believed that animal breeding began accidentally when some men lured medium-size animals to their camps to select and slaughter them.

Containers for Storage

Neolithic communities developed new techniques for storing food. They molded various objects from mud and then baked them in fire to harden them and make them more durable.

LIVESTOCK BREEDING
This began with the breeding of herbivorous animals, such as goats and sheep, which would be kept safe in pens during the colder months.

Food in the Village

The division of labor is a distinguishing feature of Neolithic settlements. Agriculture and livestock breeding required different tasks that were spaced out through the year. Sowing and harvesting were the busiest times. At the same time, people milled corn, manufactured clay containers to store it, sheared livestock, and processed meat.

PREPARATION
Clearing the land made the tasks involved in farming possible.

HARVESTING
Wheat and barley were collected at harvesttime and stored.

MILLING
Grinding corn meant that it could be stored for periods of scarcity.

1 PRODUCTION CYCLE
After harvesting, threshing began—a process of separating the grain from the chaff. Some of the grain was milled and some was kept for sowing the following year.

2 DOMESTICATION
To guarantee the reproduction of flocks and herds, preference was given to females and the young. Older, male animals would be eaten first.

3 TRANSITION
Hunting and fishing continued to be practiced in the Neolithic period; meat and fish complemented the diet and served as a backup in periods of poor harvests.

4 SOWING
Wooden plows enabled the soil to be moved more easily and larger areas of land to be worked. The use of polished stone also helped to improve tools.

WILD FRUIT
The diet was complemented with the gathering of juniper berries, elderberries, and acorns, among other things.

MEAT PREPARATION
This was usually salted and dried in the sun. Later it was roasted or boiled in soups and broths.

4

Passing on Knowledge

To guarantee their survival, early humans had to pass on to their children a whole collection of indispensable knowledge that was not included in their inherited traits but that they had learned themselves. During the Paleolithic period, knowledge and techniques were taught concerning how to make and control fire and how to use tools to hunt large animals. Later on, during the Neolithic period, more elaborate knowledge was transmitted that made possible the development of agriculture and livestock breeding.

Practical Training

In early times, education was short in duration—everything necessary was taught quickly. Youngsters would learn by doing—there was no differentiation between doing and learning. It was also omnilateral, meaning everyone learned everything and there was no specialization.

Gradually, starting with increasing complexity of knowledge, the appearance of social differentiation and the unequal appropriation of surpluses, these characteristics were lost. Education became more specialized and was conducted at specific times and in specific areas that were distinct for men and women as well as for social groups.

The first specific educational practice that was found in all the cultures of the world was the initiation rite. These ceremonies generally marked the transition from childhood to adulthood, and often left signs on the body, such as tattoos or circumcisions. They were performed at given times and places, with established roles for those performing the initiation and those undergoing it, a series of ritual elements—clothing, music, food, objects, and so on—and the teaching of certain skills considered essential in each community.

Complex Techniques

Increased social complexity allowed the development of objects that performed not only a practical but also an aesthetic function, such as these items of decoration found in Catal Hüyük in modern-day Turkey.

3

Livestock Breeding

Evidence from cave paintings, such as this one, shows that Neolithic people began to breed and keep livestock for food.

Sacred Ceremonies

Rituals in sacred sites (such as Stonehenge) were important educational acts in the Neolithic period. They were performed on occasions associated with astrological or climatic events, and participation was differentiated by gender, age, and social standing.

Group Tasks

During the Paleolithic period, hunter-gatherers typically lived in large groups. These had between twenty and forty members and were split into small groups for tasks such as hunting. Over time, they gave rise to tribes, united by family ties.

1 LEARNING BY IMITATION
Education was collective. Adults demonstrated their knowledge by example and specific action, and children accompanied and imitated them, participating in everyday activities.

2 PASSING ON KNOWLEDGE
Information and skills began to be passed from generation to generation. Adults taught children what they had learned from their parents during their childhood, and at the same time contributed the knowledge that they themselves had developed arising out of their own needs.

3 TRAINING THROUGH ACTION
The child observes how the adult fishes. He gradually joins in to then try for himself, and later teach what he has learned to his children when he is old enough.

Use of Tools

In the Paleolithic period, one of the first materials that humanity had to master was stone. Using carving and polishing techniques, humans were able to use stone as weapons to hunt and fish. Later, with the advent of agriculture, stone was used as part of a plow.

POLISHING STONES

The child tries to polish stones by copying what the adult does, while the adult helps and guides.

MATERIAL CULTURE

As people began to stay in permanent settlements, more and more tools were developed and used.

CLOSE TO WATER

Water was an essential resource for the location of settlements in early societies.

Sedentary Tasks

Ten thousand years ago, humans began to settle permanently in villages and farm the land. For the first time, because not everyone was needed to find food, trades and special jobs appeared. The possibility of working in a continuous and predictable way enabled surpluses to be produced and stored. Gradually, the accumulation of these surpluses and the diversification of jobs led to greater inequality, which resulted in hierarchical, stratified societies. As different occupations acquired differing degrees of importance, some people became more powerful than others.

New Trades

During the Paleolithic period, humans moved across environments and devoted their time to hunting and gathering. Their skills for subsistence were learned through practice—imitating the older members of the group. By around 8,000 BC, the human groups of the Neolithic period remained in stable settlements, thanks to the development of agriculture and livestock breeding. This situation brought about the development of an increasing specialization of tasks, which led to a division of labor into trades and skills. There arose manufacturers of tools, builders of houses and canals, weavers, potters, and blacksmiths, among many other specializations. The transformation was so radical that scholars now call this the "Neolithic revolution."

Early Farmers

The production of food meant better nutrition than during earlier periods and the supply of food could increase as the population gradually grew in size.

PLOWING
The first tools were made of wood.

FARMERS
People lived from their own efforts and production.

CROPS
The first cereals were rye, wheat, and barley.

Activities and Specialization

In prehistory, human beings performed a number of tasks to guarantee their survival. From the first crude stone tools (right) to the founding of metals, work became more complex and specialized in terms of the various tasks and responsibilities involved.

2,000,000 BC
CREATING TOOLS

Homo habilis manufactures stone tools, enabling him to trap animals and harvest plants and wild fruit.

200,000 BC
COMMUNITY HUNTING

Homo erectus implements systematic group hunting. His tools are sophisticated and include work in both stone and bone.

In the Home

The activities that required less physical strength were carried out by women, who prepared the food, took care of the children, and made clothes.

MILLING
Flour was made by grinding seeds with stones.

FABRICS

Material was woven from wool provided by domesticated sheep.

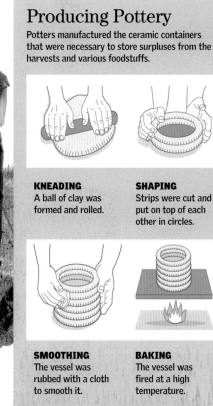

Producing Pottery

Potters manufactured the ceramic containers that were necessary to store surpluses from the harvests and various foodstuffs.

KNEADING
A ball of clay was formed and rolled.

SHAPING
Strips were cut and put on top of each other in circles.

SMOOTHING
The vessel was rubbed with a cloth to smooth it.

BAKING
The vessel was fired at a high temperature.

Blacksmiths

Over time, the production of tools became more complex with the use of metals: first copper, then bronze, and finally iron. They were shaped by hammering or founding.

HAMMERING
Metals could be shaped with hammer blows.

WARRIORS
Metals transformed warfare.

FOUNDING
The metal was poured into the mold to solidify.

50,000 BC
MAKING CLOTHES

The Ice Age prompted the manufacture of clothes. Skins and hides served as cover and protection against a hostile, unpredictable climate.

20,000 BC
FIRST ARTISTS

Paleolithic artists reflected their understanding of the world in wall paintings located in caves and in small sculptures made from clay or stone.

8000 BC
PRODUCTIVE WORK

The domestication of animals and agricultural practices expanded in the Fertile Crescent. Milling was done manually with stone mortars.

2000 BC
WORKING METALS

Skill in smelting metals, especially iron (left), gave comparative advantages in the various wars in the Near East.

Prehistoric Markets

The Paleolithic period—the Stone Age that lasted almost three million years, in which humankind went from being one of a number of migratory species of hominid to living in permanent settlements and farming the land—was also undoubtedly when people began to trade goods. But it was only during the Neolithic period, with the advent of the first civilizations, that trade began to really take shape. It is possible that trade was initially based on a system of bartering.

Radical Changes

When humankind learned to cultivate the land and breed livestock, they ceased to be hunter-gatherers and began to settle in towns. This happened around 10,000 years ago. One of the first profound consequences of this radical change in their way of life was the creation of surpluses—that is, the capacity to produce greater quantities of food than were consumed. The best option was to exchange this valuable surplus for other necessary goods: other types of food, tools, and beasts of burden. This meant the birth of commerce, which led suddenly to the creation of new roles, and to society being split into social strata. Now some people could devote themselves solely to manufacturing tools, for example, which they could later exchange for food. At the same time, owners of the most valued items in society began to occupy the highest strata of their community.

Current Example

An example of the gift economy still occurs in some tribal societies, for example, when the hunters share their prey with the rest of the community.

FOOD
The way that food was produced led to changes in social structure.

Pottery

The Neolithic period also brought about a major development in pottery. Containers, the product of this development, were used to store and transport goods. Ceramic pots were also used to cook food, which contributed to improving the health of communities.

New Relations

Trade prompted the people of the community to relate to each other in different ways, including the following:

BARTERING
Objects and services were exchanged.

TASKS
People began to specialize in one skill or trade.

SETTLEMENTS
Humankind ceased to be nomadic.

artering Questioned

 a long time, it was believed that the economy he Neolithic period was based on bartering. ever, some authors question this, or at least use on a large scale. Bartering requires a cidence of desires: "I want what you have rplus of, and vice versa." For this reason, y it is usually considered that it was the gift nomy that predominated at that time, which sists of giving instead of selling goods.

New Tools

New tools speeded up development in the Neolithic period and were also valuable objects to exchange.

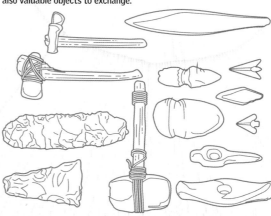

Urban Settlement

The fortress city of Catal Hüyük stood on a fertile plain called Konya, in modern-day Turkey, from around 7,000 BC. Its population was made up of farmers who cultivated wheat, beans, lentils, and barley around the settlement. This town was composed of a conglomerate of little dwellings huddled together, which had the peculiarity of having their entrance doors on their roofs. The walls of the houses were built of mud bricks that, as time passed, usually collapsed, giving rise to the formation of an artificial hill.

Groups of Small Houses

The dwellings were distributed into small neighborhoods. In turn, each of these had a central patio, which served as a bathroom and a garbage dump. The waste and garbage was burned in the open air.

WOOD AND REED COVERINGS

The roofs of the houses were made using wooden strips, which were covered with reed mats and layers of mud rolled flat on the upper part.

RAW MATERIAL

The mud used for construction was sun-baked mud bricks. The raw material was extracted from the Casamba River, near the town.

OPEN AIR

During the hottest periods, the population carried out their daily activities—such as weaving, making baskets and tools, and eating—under the roofs.

NOT MUCH LIGHT

The openings were small and were located in the eaves. Their size and arrangement meant that as little cold as possible entered in the winter.

TERRACES

Since streets did not exist and the dwellings were built huddled together, the population walked on the roofs. Together, they formed an open space similar to a plaza. It is supposed that large communal ovens were also built on these terraces.

1 DAILY COOKING
Small rectangular stoves or clay ovens were used to cook the food and heat the rooms.

2 COMFORTABLE SLEEP
The walls had two rectangular platforms against them, which were used for sitting and sleeping. Likewise, similar platforms were used as shelves on which to place belongings.

3 STORAGE
The dwellings had a small room that was used to store food and tools.

4 PLASTERED WALLS
As a form of preservation, the inside and outside walls were covered with plaster.

5 SHRINES
There were rooms with bull heads made of plaster with authentic horns. It is believed that the people worshipped their gods there.

6 BEAUTIFUL PAINTINGS
Some internal walls were decorated with paintings depicting scenes of wild animals and men hunting.

Siting and Decline

Catal Hüyük was located on a hillock around 66 feet (20 meters) high, surrounded by a wide plain. In around 5000 BC, the town was suddenly abandoned. Archaeologists suppose that a sudden climatic change could be the most likely explanation for this historical puzzle.

The Big City is Born

The Sumerians lived in Asian Mesopotamia, the region between the Tigris and Euphrates rivers, in what today is Iraq. They are considered the first great civilization in history, due to their outstanding developments in urban planning and their pioneering contributions to the sphere of knowledge. They took advantage of the resources that nature provided, making dwellings with adobe (bricks made of sun-dried mud) and inventing irrigation for agriculture. For worship, they built imposing temples called ziggurats.

Urbanism

The most significant and lasting innovation of Sumerian civilization was urbanism. At the end of the third millennium BC, 90 percent of the population of southern Mesopotamia lived in cities and towns. This characteristic aroused both the admiration and greed of invaders.

OUTSIDE WALLS

The walls were smooth and whitish in color. Windows were not used and the rooms had little natural light.

INSULATION

Adobe bricks were used, which enabled heat to be retained during the night but kept the house cool during hotter days.

RECEPTION

Adjacent to the entrance door, a small antechamber protected the inside of the house.

Ziggurat

Sumerian architecture reached its height in the ziggurat, a pyramid-shaped temple consisting of a number of terraces built on top of each other and a ceremonial enclosure right at the top. They were up to 50 feet (15 meters) in height and constructed using adobe bricks. Their quadrangular base could measure up to 200 feet (60 meters) on each side.

1 DAILY LIFE
The houses did not follow a regular plan, although it was normal for them to have roofs that could be walked on to take advantage of the light from above.

2 FLOOR LAYOUT
Sumerian dwellings could be circular or rectangular. However, they all had an open central space, allowing each bedroom to receive light and ventilation.

3 CORRIDORS
In the dwellings that had two floors, the upstairs rooms could communicate by means of a continuous balcony. Because wood was scarce, this corridor was generally made with solid matting or reeds.

4 SIMPLICITY
Most furniture was made of wickerwork. The tables were usually low, because people normally sat on the floor. To sleep, they lay on the floor or on simple mats.

5 FAMILY FOOD
Each dwelling had an area dedicated to the preparation of food. A clay oven was placed there, which was used to bake bread—the basis of nutrition. In general, the meat that was consumed came from farmyard poultry.

6 STARTING AGAIN
Foundations were not used, because the soil was heavy clay. When a construction was no longer safe, it was torn down and rebuilt on the same site.

Ingenious Construction

The first Sumerian houses were cylindrical and were built with bundles of dry cane and reed. It is supposed that they could have been occupied by a number of families at the same time. This type of construction is still used today, and is called a *mudhif*.

MAIN MATERIAL

Stone was scarce in the region and the wood was not very good. That is why the Sumerians built using adobe bricks, made with mud. The problem with this was that, due to factors such as the wind and rain, the bricks disintegrated after a while.

The Law of Men

Domestic life in ancient Asian Mesopotamia was characterized by the father or head of the family holding maximum authority. His power was considered to be lifelong and was passed on to the eldest son from marriage after the father's death. Monogamy—in other words, the existence of a single marriage union between a man and a woman—was the predominant form of marital arrangement. However, the importance of the male heir meant it was possible for men to take a second wife to guarantee the line of descent. Marriages were sometimes dissolved, but only on the husband's initiative. Daughters did not inherit but received a dowry when they married in unions agreed upon by their fathers.

Respecting the Master

The history of the family in Asian Mesopotamia involved a heterogeneous set of customs corresponding to various peoples: Sumerians, Akkadians, Babylonians, Assyrians, and Persians. Aside from cultural differences, the asymmetry of roles within the family was customary in established relations: the women and children always had to respect the decisions of the head of the family. The monogamic system was completed by the notion of the extended family; this means that, in addition to the married couple and their unmarried children,

close relatives or some married sons and their children, among others, would be included. The privileged members of society, such as monarchs and state officials, demonstrated the strongest expression of male authority: there were only men in politics.

MOTHERHOOD
Husbands and sons had to respect their mothers. The women were responsible for feeding and making clothes for the children.

TOTAL AUTHORITY
The father, or *album*, supervised the teaching of the children.

Mesopotamian Marriage
The marriage union was formally registered in front of the state authorities without any need for witnesses. They were able to record the union using cuneiform script (engraving with wedge-shape characters) on clay tablets.

THE DOWRY
A dowry was the wealth that the bride's father gave to the husband at the time of the marriage. If the marriage was dissolved, the husband had to return the gifts along with his wife.

Family Verticalism

The wishes of the head of the family were respected above all else in the Mesopotamian home. However, this authority also implied obligations for the man, such as respecting the physical well-being of and supporting his wife and children.

1 SLAVERY
The use of slaves was widespread in Asian Mesopotamia. Only highly trusted servants would work with the wives in the tasks of weaving and caring for the children.

2 FEMALES
The wives and daughters belonged to the private domestic domain; they were not seen in public and did not take part in meetings.

3 GUARDS
As in all hereditary monarchies, the kings and the members of their families were closely protected.

4 MALE WORLD
Nondomestic matters, especially political issues, were the exclusive sphere of the male population.

The Mesopotamian Woman

A woman passed from the tutelage of her father to that of her husband. Women had rights, but these were inferior to those of men.

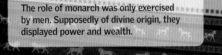

MONARCH, FATHER, AND POWER
The role of monarch was only exercised by men. Supposedly of divine origin, they displayed power and wealth.

TASTY DISHES
The food was prepared by servants of both sexes, who resided in the palaces of the powerful.

ASYMMETRY
The absence of equality characterized society and family relations throughout Mesopotamia.

OFFICIALS
Their duty was to be totally loyal to the absolute monarch.

NO FREEDOM
Servants were denied rights of any kind.

Men of Iron

From the late tenth century BC to the seventh century BC, the Assyrian Empire dominated the whole of the ancient Near East: it stretched from Mesopotamia in the east, passing through Palestine, to Egypt in the west. Even if it took such an empire—for various reasons—after reaching its zenith, just fifty years to crumble, its creation was based on formidable might in war. Warriors both cruel and courageous, skilled horse riders, and archers, the Assyrians combined their natural capacities for combat, organization, efficiency, and discipline. This turned them into the first military power in history and into one of the best-organized armies until the appearance of the Roman legions.

By Divine Mandate

The roots of Assyrian militarism are to be found in a combination of geographical and religious factors. Assyria had fertile land, on which the most precious commodity of the age was cultivated: corn. Due to the absence of natural boundaries, such as rivers or mountains, that might make its frontiers defendable, this land became too attractive and accessible a booty for other peoples. That is why Assyria had to create a sufficiently powerful army to anticipate any attempt at invasion, and undertook devastating campaigns against those who might prove a threat. The other military motivation was religious in nature. The Assyrians believed that their god Ashur had given them the mission to unify under his command the entire known world. And, once other peoples were conquered, the army had to keep these dominions under control, placing garrisons at strategic points in the conquered lands. Meanwhile the core of the army was held in reserve under the command of the king, ready to be mobilized in the event of war or a new campaign.

Shock Force

The Assyrian army was the first to use large cavalry squadrons. The chariots acted as a genuine shock force: they carried four warriors and the horses were protected with leather armor.

Special Troops

This army was composed of 200,000 men.
The finest were in its excellent cavalry.
Furthermore, it was made up of heavy and
light infantry, armed mostly with spears and
shields; shock groups made up of archers
and slingshot throwers; and assault troops,
sappers, and engineers.

Assyrian Weapons

The Assyrians had a key advantage over their
adversaries: their iron weapons, which were
much superior to the bronze ones that were still
widely used during this period. The Assyrians
were also outstanding in siege warfare, and
created special machines for that purpose.

MASTERS OF SIEGE

Experts in besieging
cities, they used
machines such
as the battering
ram and the
assault tower.

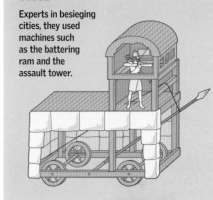

HEAVY CAVALRY
The Assyrian cavalry
used 3,000 horses
per month.

SLINGSHOT THROWERS
Their function was to
harass the enemy. Their
shots were lethal.

HEAVY INFANTRY
Heavily armed, it
was the infantry who
defined the outcome
of battles.

ARCHERS
The first mounted
archers in the world,
the Assyrians shot
arrows at a gallop.

ARROW AND QUIVER

The design of the arrow
they introduced in around
1800 BC allowed them to
fire from a horse.

MACES

The maces had iron heads.
Officers used them as a
staff of authority.

SHIELD BEARER
There were two shield
bearers: one to protect
the archer and the other
to protect the driver from
enemy projectiles.

HORSES
The four horses gave Assyrian
chariots their shock power.

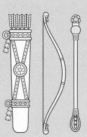

Ancient Egypt

The Nile River, which flows about 4,130 miles (6,650 kilometers) through Africa to the Mediterranean Sea, allowed the ancient Egyptian civilization to survive, grow, and thrive. Ancient Egyptians lived along the banks of the lower reaches of the Nile, where fertile land let them grow crops and raise animals,

with evidence of settlements dating back to 5000 BC. The river also provided water and was the major mode of transportation. Two separate kingdoms developed along the Nile: Upper Egypt (*Ta-Shemau*) and Lower Egypt (*Ta-Mehu*). In ca. 3200 BC, the northern pharaoh, Menes, conquered the south and unified Egypt.

A Family Cell

Ancient Egyptian dwellings were constructed from bricks and clay, and housed large extended families consisting of parents, grandparents, uncles, and aunts, as well as four or five children, on average. Some families also had pets. The majority of the population lived in the countryside in small hamlets close to the fields under cultivation. These were by the banks of the legendary Nile River. The rooms had distinct functions, and the basements were used as much as the flat roofs. Egyptians even had a living room where family members shared meals, work, and free time. The windows of these dwellings were high up in the walls to keep out the sun as well as dirt and sand. The white walls were decorated with geometric and pictorial motifs, and inside these family cells was some sophisticated furniture, including beds and armchairs.

Essential Clay

The Egyptians, like other contemporary civilizations, made the most of soil as a raw material. They sun-dried it in wooden molds to create bricks, which, covered with bitumen, were rendered waterproof against rainfall.

VENTILATION

These houses had air vents on the roofs. They also had windows on the upper part of the outside walls, which were small, rectangular openings without glass.

HARD OUTSIDE WALLS

The walls were solid clay-brick structures mounted on stone foundations.

INITIAL ENTRY

The outer door was much thicker than those inside, and had a system of security locks. It was made of wood.

SECURITY

Because the windows did not have glass, bars or stone grilles were used in order to prevent animals or strangers from entering. Valuable objects were usually kept in the basement—the most inaccessible room in the dwelling.

1 WELCOME

The hall was the dwelling's main entrance area, where people from outside the family unit were received. Usually it was profusely decorated, featuring an altar in honor of the god Bes—protector of the family, children, and pregnant women.

2 COOKING

Kitchens were well equipped, with spaces for the safekeeping of cutlery and cooking utensils, such as ladles, pots, and pitchers of different types. There were also mortars and mud ovens, where bread with yeast, among other things, was made.

3 BASEMENT

The basement was used especially for storing food, which included onions, vegetables, radishes, and fruit. It was not easy to get into the basement, because its entrance was always concealed or covered with some kind of cover or hatch.

4 DUTIES

The Egyptians devoted most of the day to work. They also dried and salted meat and fish on the roofs before they ate it.

BEDS

Beds could be simple rush mats unfolded on the floor, or actual beds made from braided hemp with a headrest of decorated wood.

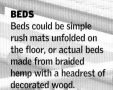

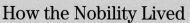

FAMILY AREA AND FURNITURE

In this central room, family members saw each other every day. They had stools, armchairs, tables, and ceramic pitchers. The best pieces of furniture were wooden, with carvings and pictures.

How the Nobility Lived

The families closest to the pharaoh, or the most powerful Egyptians, built dwellings with large gardens and patios, where they grew flowers, plants, and palm trees. They even used to build pools, where they could cool down in the intense desert heat. Sometimes certain families chose to have an interior patio, which became the center of the house; this supplied light and lessened the intensity of the sun's rays.

Sacred Union

Family ties were highly respected in ancient Egyptian society. The composition of the family and the admiration in which it was held took inspiration from the legend of Osiris, a divinity who had received unwavering love from Isis, his wife, and eternal faithfulness and respect from Horus, his son. Neither religious nor civil authorities participated in the celebration of Egyptian marriage, because this ceremony was considered a voluntary and private act; the bride and groom started family life once they decided to go and live together. The couple got engaged while young, and families were large; they had many children because of the very high infant mortality rate.

Social Inequality

The pharaoh was head of a theocratic government in which he was considered to be a god. As such, the royal family was at the top of the social hierarchy and was the sector with the greatest privileges. The nobles were maintained by the whole population, and they dedicated their time to recreation by means of games, feasts, and different activities. Marriages within royalty were endogamous—that is, they chose their spouses from within their kinship group. For example, men who were heirs to the throne married one of their sisters to assure dynastic continuity. Peasant families made up the majority of the population. They lived in humble abodes and were obliged to work hard to pay the state taxes. Monogamy was most widely practiced, and polygamy (union with more than one individual) could be found only in the highest levels of society. In any case, both conjugal methods were related more to practical than to moral issues; for example, the need for descendants or the right to inherit for both men and women. Slaves were prohibited from getting married.

HABITAT
The living room was decorated with natural motifs, such as papyrus and lotus flowers, from the Nile River.

Maternity and Cleanliness

Women were responsible for washing the hands of their family members; first, on getting up, and then during meals. The bathroom equipment usually consisted of a portable receptacle and a pitcher. The Egyptians took great care both of their bodies and of the general cleanliness of their homes.

PLAY
Egyptian tombs preserved numerous models of ancient wooden toys, such as this one.

Any Afternoon

Free time within the family was highly valued by the Egyptians. There were numerous ingenious and entertaining board games, which were widespread among the population. State officials tended to have access to the greatest resources and were often able to provide their families with some comforts, as well as servants and extras things that other groups did not have.

1 LEISURE TIME
Senet was the most widespread board game in ancient Egypt, among both nobles and ordinary people.

3 PETS
Cats and poultry were preferred as pets. They were cared for, loved, and even mummified in tombs.

2 FEMALE INSTRUCTION
Mothers were in charge of the education of boys and girls. There was utmost respect for both maternal and paternal authority.

4 REST
Beds were narrow and made on small mats. Married couples did not normally share a bed.

SHAVED HEADS
Everyone shaved their heads to protect themselves from lice, and wealthier Egyptians had wigs and hairpieces.

MARRIAGE
A powerful man could have several wives, but the first wife was in charge of running the house.

CHILDREN
Children were all equally doted upon, and many learned to read and write.

On the Way to Equality

Women longed for motherhood in ancient Egypt. Children were considered a divine blessing, and for that reason abortion was forbidden by law. Daughters were wanted as much as sons, and between the ages of fourteen and forty women gave birth, on average, to eight children. The high rate of infant mortality meant that only around half of them survived. With regard to the role of women within society, although the man had overall control within the family, Egyptian women enjoyed numerous rights because they had legal autonomy. As an example of this, even though the eldest male would inherit, women could trade and manage their own goods, which they might have received as gifts or for personal work.

Caring for the Family

Medical knowledge in Egyptian society meant it was a deep-rooted principle in the Nile territories for families to take care of their health. Although both men and women looked after their physical appearance and the general condition of their bodies, it was mothers who supervised their own children's health care.

To find out whether women were pregnant, the ancient Egyptians would pour some drops of urine into a container with grains of wheat and into another with barley. If the seeds germinated after a few days, it meant that there was a pregnancy. The birth was left in the hands of midwives or, in difficult or special cases, a doctor. Birth was a kind of ritual in which the woman was bathed with olive oil to aid her relaxation. Childbirth took place in a room in the house called the "birth pavilion." The mother had to crouch down during labor, and the midwives worked while reciting magic formulae to protect the life of the newborn child.

1 LIBERTY OF ACTION
The Egyptians respected women. They could choose their work and follow their occupational callings.

2 PHYSICAL APPEARANCE
In murals, the female body was usually shown as slim, graceful, and well cared for, while the male body was of strong build.

3 UNFAZED
The Egyptians were proud of their physical appearance. Women usually wore transparent clothes, which highlighted their natural shape.

Women And Power

Nefertiti was the wife and coregent of the Pharaoh Akhenaton. After her reign, women from the privileged sectors started to appear in works of art beside their husbands and descendants.

MAKING BEAUTIFUL

Necklaces, headdresses, earrings, and bracelets were commonly worn by Egyptian women. The richest women used gold as a raw material.

SELF-RECOGNITION

The oldest mirrors in history were of Egyptian origin, showing a desire to look good and maintain physical beauty.

Leading Role in Society

Unquestionably, Egyptian women left an impression. In Egyptian tombs, religious scenes and funerary rituals were enlivened by numerous female figures. They were represented in dances, at feasts, or at work.

AESTHETICS
For reasons of hygiene and aesthetics, women removed their body hair.

MAKEUP
Cosmetic ointments were made of ground minerals. A blackish color for the eyes was obtained from galena, a lead ore.

HAIR AND HAIRSTYLES
It was typical for women to dye their hair with henna, a natural red-colored dye.

EMPLOYMENT OF SERVANTS
The wealthiest Egyptian families had servants dedicated to washing their clothes and keeping their wigs in good condition.

Bread—A Sacred Food

The periodic flooding of the Nile deposited a natural fertilizer called silt on its banks. However, the Egyptians attributed this fertility to the sacredness of the river and thanked the gods for the productivity of their lands. The main crops that they harvested were cereals. Wheat allowed for the baking of bread, most people's staple diet, while barley favored the production of beer, an essential Egyptian drink.

Agricultural Prosperity

The ancient Egyptians believed that their gods were responsible for the success or failure of their crops and harvests. Independent of their religious ideas, we know that they achieved three annual harvests, thanks to the construction of a widespread system of dikes and canals distributed along the length of the Nile River. Both humans and nature contributed to the abundance of food. Cereals, such as wheat and barley, were the essential agricultural products. The ancient Egyptians grew legumes and vegetables, such as celery, watercress, asparagus, lettuce, garlic, onions, chickpeas, and lentils. The most popular fruits were dates, figs, grapes, apples, and melons.

Although the whole population frequently ate bread and drank beer, dietary habits varied significantly among the social groups. Those who were more privileged ate all kinds of foods, and meat from farm animals and birds formed a large proportion of their diet. On the other hand, the majority of the population did not eat meat because it was expensive to keep herds. Peasants could eat beef only on festival days, when cattle were sacrificed in the temples and the meat was distributed among the people. Birds and fish, obtained from hunting and fishing, were more often eaten.

Food as Tax

The pharaoh's granaries were located throughout Egypt. Special officials carried out the tasks of organizing collection and storing the harvested cereals.

HUNTING AND FISHING

Agriculture was complemented by bird hunting and by fishing on the banks of the Nile River. Paté was made from goose liver.

DRINKS

Beer was the most common drink in ancient Egypt. Wine, on the other hand, was more commonly associated with the dietary habits of the nobility.

THE USE OF FLAX

Different kinds of flax were cultivated. It was used in food, and also as material for making clothes.

Making Bread

The Egyptians discovered how to use yeast as well as the process of fermentation. This made them pioneers in the art of making bread. In the dwellings of well-to-do families, kitchens were situated at a distance from the other rooms to keep away the heat from the ovens. People without ovens took the dough to a communal oven. Each group of families had a uniquely formed mold to identify it.

 DISTRIBUTION
After the harvest, one portion of the grain was set aside for tax; another part was reserved for the next sowing; and the last was separated for milling.

 MILLING
Usually, only women dedicated themselves to milling the grain. They patiently ground it until they had the flour necessary for making the bread.

 MIXING
The flour was moistened and mixed with yeast. It was kneaded by hand in a wicker basket, until the required consistency was reached for baking.

WATER
This was either stored in stone wells or was carried every day from the banks of the river.

INSIDE TASKS
Grain was treated in a dry environment, protected from the sun's rays.

INSIDE TASKS
Grain was treated in a dry environment, protected from the sun's rays.

OUTSIDE TASKS
The houses of the elite had a patio for the oven, while, in contrast, the poor cooked on their flat roofs.

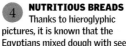 **NUTRITIOUS BREADS**
Thanks to hieroglyphic pictures, it is known that the Egyptians mixed dough with seeds from different plants, with the purpose of making the bread more nutritious.

 BAKING
Cooks did not have coal at their disposal; they only had wood. Meanwhile, those who had animals used the dry excrement as a fuel.

Learning to Write

One of humanity's first civilizations, that of the ancient Egyptians, developed on the banks of the Nile River, in northern Africa, in approximately 5000 BC. A complex society arose, with a theocratic political organization that was centered on the pharaoh. Widespread economic activity allowed it to achieve important cultural successes in architecture, engineering, agriculture, and other fields. The Egyptians stood out for their advances in mathematics, medicine, and astronomy. Their most important cultural contribution was the invention of one of the first methods of writing, hieroglyphics, which was based on images representing ideas, beliefs, or proper names.

Education in the Temples

In Egypt, education was broadly related to culture and religion. After being taught within the family environment, six- and seven-year-old boys entered a separate type of school for village boys and sons of officials. There, they were taught about reading, writing, and calculus. Then the basics in geometry and astronomy were added, as well as gymnastic exercises. The upper schools were in the temples, and were attended until the age of seventeen by those being prepared for posts such as scribes or state officials.

Although they were open to everyone, it was mainly young people from the well-to-do classes who attended, because those from the poorest sectors had to start their working life. Many of these schools operated as boarding schools run by priests, which shows how closely education and religion were connected in this culture. Training in the schools was very comprehensive: hieroglyphic writing and hieratic script were taught, as were the principles of administration and accounting, and ideas about technology and art. Also studied in more depth were subjects such as mathematics, astronomy, fine art, sculpture, poetry, and dance.

Egyptian Alphabet

The symbols of the Egyptian alphabet represent concepts ranging from simple and complex elements, to procedures, astronomical objects, and periods of time. The system is based on ideograms and made up of consonants.

DIRECTION OF READING

Scripts were read the direction in which animal heads were facing.

S Y   L   L   P
   M   O   T

HIEROGLYPHIC WRITING

This wording reads from right to left and refers to Ptolemy, the Egyptian king. Experts were able to decipher it after the Rosetta Stone was found.

Lessons Within the Family

The first lessons were received within the heart of the family and were based on the teaching of religious and moral precepts, general care, hygiene, discipline, and obedience.

PAPYRUS
This was kept rolled up in baskets or in ceramic jars.

School for Scribes

The officials with responsibility for writing, accounting, and the copying and classification of state documents were the scribes. The profession was transmitted from father to son, so they ended up comprising a special caste. Their training was complex and was carried out in specific schools.

RITUAL

Before starting a task, the students said a prayer to Tot, their patron god, and placed themselves under his protection and care.

1 POSTURE
One of the first things that scribes learned was to sit in a special position for carrying out a task.

3 FIRST COPIES
The new students started their practice by making copies of short texts presented by the teacher.

5 LIMESTONE AND CERAMICS
Because papyrus was expensive, pupils started by copying phrases on fragments of limestone or ceramic.

2 WORK MATERIAL
The papyrus was made by smoothing and pressing fibers of a plant of the same name, which grew on the Nile.

4 MASTER SCRIBE
Only a person who had been trained as a professional scribe in a specialized school could take on the role of teacher.

The Scribe Amenemope

Amenemope lived in the Ancient Empire and left guidelines for the professional training of sons, at that time the responsibility of their fathers.

6 TOOLS
As training advanced, reeds, dye, mortar, water, and papyrus were used.

BOYS
The task of scribe was considered to be an exclusively male activity.

SHAVED HEADS
Students were shaved to help combat the prevailing heat.

The Pyramid of Cheops

If there is one type of construction that has become a universal symbol of ancient Egypt, it is the pyramid. Indeed, for the whole world the empire of the Nile is "the country of pyramids." This model of construction has, in turn, become the symbol of a society governed by a centralist, hierarchical, and vertical power—a "pyramidal society"—such as that which dominated in ancient Egypt. Of all the pyramids, there is one that without doubt is the most emblematic: the Pyramid of Cheops—a colossal work of engineering, whose mysteries have still not been completely revealed. Constructed in the reign of Cheops, between 2551 and 2528 BC, it is the only one of the seven wonders of the ancient world that has entirely survived the passage of time.

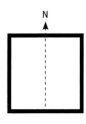

N

DIMENSIONS
It is taller than the Pyramid of Kefren (471 feet/143.5 meters) and the Pyramid of Micerino (328 feet/ 100 meters).

Height: 481 feet (146.6 meters)

Base: 755 feet (230 meters)

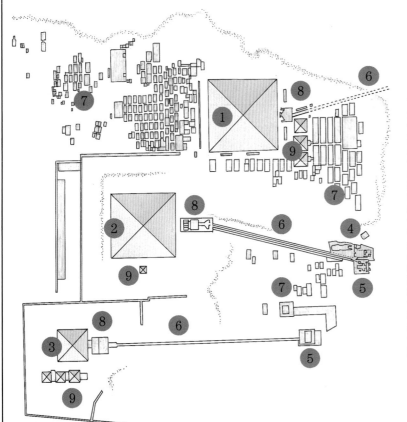

City of the Dead

The Valley of Giza is an immense necropolis on the west bank of the Nile River. It harbors the three most outstanding pyramids from the Egypt of the pharaohs: namely those at Cheops (1), Kefren (2), and Micerino (3). Each pyramid forms part of a mortuary complex, in which, with the exception of the Great Sphinx and also a sculpture in the pyramid at Kefren (4), the same elements are repeated. Moreover, in the valley stands the Great Temple (5), the so-called "Procession Route" (6), the dignitary's *mastaba* (7), the funerary temples (8), and other pyramids (9).

THE QUEEN'S TOMB
Despite what its name suggests, this compartment holds the funerary possessions of Cheops. His wife is buried in an adjoining pyramid.

SUBTERRANEAN CHAMBER
This chamber is an unfinished and empty room, which could be a decoy to dissuade the tomb raiders, or a possible site, later rejected, for the sarcophagus.

Development of Funerary Temples

MASTABA
The first tombs of the noble Egyptians were subterranean funerary chambers, on top of which a chapel consisting of just one floor was constructed for offerings and religious rituals.

PYRAMID
Pyramids arose from the superposition of different floors in the mastabas. The Pyramid of Dashur, one of the oldest, contains evidence of initial problems in achieving the definitive pyramidal form.

HIPOGEO
The hipogeo was the Theban pharaoh's response to the plundering of the pyramid treasures. The funerary chamber and the chapel were hidden in caves dug out below ground, or into bare rock.

TOMB OF THE PHARAOH
This funerary chamber covers some 538 square feet (50 square meters) and, because it has been mercilessly plundered, it harbors only one empty sarcophagus of red granite. The weight of the blocks that make up the roof is supported by five compartments. In one of those are written the names of two groups of slaves who worked on the construction.

GREAT FIND
In September 2002, a robot demonstrated that the ventilation conduits, possibly conceived as routes for the pharaoh's spirit, led to doors and chambers, which until that moment had been unknown.

SUMMIT OF GOLD
The Pyramid of Cheops was finished off with white limestone brought from the Nile. This material was capped with shiny metal, probably gold, so that the summit would reflect the sun.

MAIN GALLERY
The function of this antechamber was to connect the ascending corridor with the Pharaoh's tomb. Its dimensions were 151 feet (46 meters) in length, by 28 feet (8.5 meters).

THE ENTRANCE
Situated at a height of 56 feet (17 meters), the entrance was sealed by stone blocks behind the pharaoh's grave. It communicates with a subterranean chamber by a downward sloping corridor 95 feet (29 meters) long.

GRADUAL GROWTH
During the lifetime of the pharaoh, because he was advancing in age, steps covered in limestone were added, together with more rooms on the original floor; this formed the pit and nucleus of the pyramid.

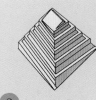

System of Ramps
The methods used in the construction of the pyramids are still the subject of intense discussion among researchers. Recent archaeological findings suggest the use of a varied system of ramps, by means of which the stone blocks could be moved up to higher levels.

1 Multiple Ramps
2 Perimeter Ramp
3 Graded Ramp
4 Single Frontal Ramp

In Honor of the Gods

The main celebrations in ancient Egypt were religious in character, and the state, headed by the pharaoh, played an active role. The Beautiful Feast of Opet took place annually, in the season when the Nile River overflowed. It consisted of a procession, which went from the Temple of Amon in Karnak, southward to the Temple of Amon in Thebes (Luxor today), covering around 2 miles (3 kilometers). It was a festival of fertility and regeneration, and it reaffirmed the divine nature of the pharaoh, who, in a ritual, received vital energy from Amon himself. The Beautiful Feast is documented from the time of Pharaoh Hatshepsut, who governed during the fifteenth century BC.

Ritual Changes

The Beautiful Feast of Opet and the Beautiful Feast of the Valley were the most important and sumptuous Egyptian celebrations. To begin with, the pilgrimage of Opet was made only with the statue of Amon, suitably protected in a ceremonial boat. Later, the pilgrims also included statues of his consort, Mut, and his son, Khonsu. In the times of Hatshepsut and his successor Tuthmosis III, the entourage, accompanied by a crowd, moved on land along the "Avenue of the Sphinxes," which connected Karnak directly with Luxor. The return journey was made by boat along the Nile River. In the times of Rameses II, both the outward and return journeys were made on the river. The festival lasted twelve days in Hatshepsut's period, and had increased to twenty-seven days around the time of Rameses II. Amon's statue remained for twenty-four days in Luxor, before its return to Karnak.

MUSIC
Musicians played stringed instruments, percussion, and wind instruments.

Fertility Celebration

From the beginnings of humanity, fertility celebrations have been linked to a deep sense of the sacred. On the left is a statuette from the Hacilar of Anatolia culture (Turkey, 7000 BC). On the right is the Hal Saflieni Hypogeum from 2500 BC, the only surviving prehistoric subterranean temple.

Luxor Temple

In its present form, Luxor Temple was constructed by Amenhotep III, father of the famous Akenaton, who governed in the first half of the fourteenth century BC. Later, Rameses II created important additions. On its return journey to Karnak, and in the midst of the festivities, the boat of Amon made its way through the striking entrance to the temple.

1 THE SPHINXES
The double line of sphinxes was made—in its current form—in the time of Nectanebo I, who ruled in the fourth century BC.

2 THE PHARAOH
Accompanied by the queen consort, he led the course of the entourage, amid expressions of joy from the people.

3 THE PRIESTS
Covered with leopard skins, the priests walked in front of the boat of the god, singing sacred songs.

4 THE BOAT OF THE GOD
The statue of Amon, in a ritual boat, was carried by priests with masks that represent gods.

5 THE COLOSSI
Two large statues, about 50 feet (15 meters) high and with the face of Rameses II, watched over the entrance to the temple.

ONLOOKERS
They shared large loaves of bread, pitchers of beer, and other food among the crowd.

FEMALE DANCERS
Women danced around the entourage to the sound of music. They also performed acrobatics.

Ancient Greece

The earliest Greek civilizations date from around 4,000 years ago, with "ancient Greece" referring to the period of history that lasted from 750 BC to 146 BC (the date of the Roman conquest). The ancient Greek culture of this time is credited with providing the foundations upon which

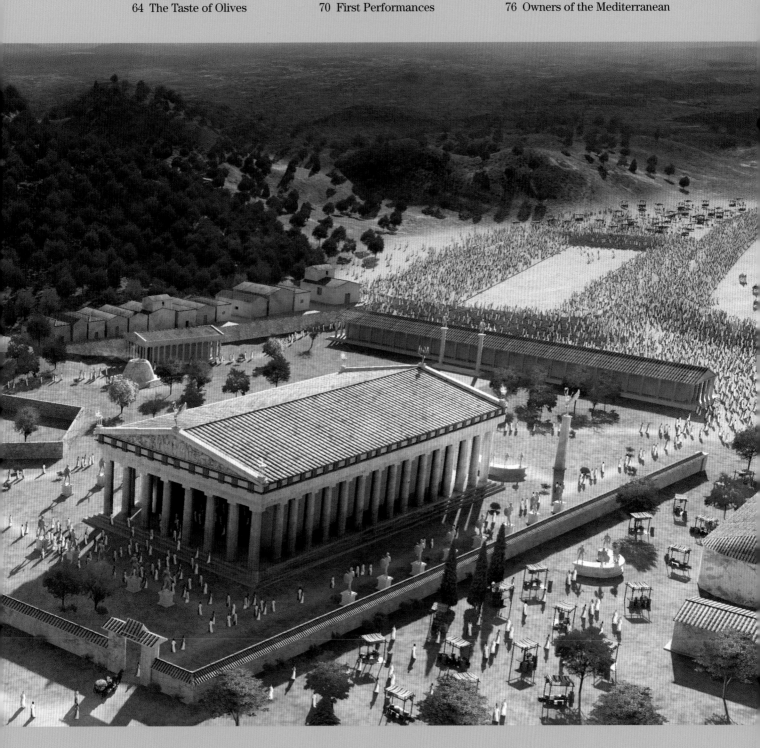

modern Western civilization is built. City-states (*poleis*), such as Athens, Sparta, and Thebes, were discrete political units with their own laws and policies and were overseen by nascent democratic governments made up of eligible citizens who had come through a rigorous education system.

Ordered Dwellings

The most powerful Greek families constructed comfortable and spacious dwellings in the Hellenistic period, which began in the fourth century BC. Most of these were located in rural areas close to busy urban centers. The domestic spaces were precisely demarcated according to sex, age, and activity. The predominant materials were wood and clay, thus making them markedly different from the monumental public constructions of marble and stone. Meanwhile, poorer people built small houses that lacked a clear design, because the quantity and layout of rooms were affected by the unevenness and extent of the land they could use.

Building According to Necessity

Greek cities lacked a regulating urban plan. For that reason, each owner constructed their dwelling according to their needs and possible options. They usually settled for a simple appearance. Houses known as *oikos* had one or two floors.

Internal Layout

Each room was assigned a particular use: there was a service area, a reception, bedrooms, a kitchen, and an area dedicated to hygiene. Later, this distinction between spaces was adopted by the Romans and expanded throughout Europe. It established the basis for Western houses today.

Functional Simplicity

In their origins, Greek city-state houses were very basic and had only one multifunctional setting. As the centuries passed, the rooms multiplied and were joined together to create larger spaces, while a central patio or garden orchard was included to provide light and ventilation.

PROTECTING THE HOME
There were few windows, and they were situated high up to protect family privacy. The openings were simple holes, square or round, which were covered with wood or fabric on cold or very windy days.

HOMEGROWN PRODUCE
Food was prepared in an area assigned as the kitchen and pantry. Poorer people prepared foodstuffs that they would eat from a portable brazier outside the home.

1

1 **THE *GYNAECEUM***
Reserved for the women and children, the *gynaeceum* was situated on the upper floor in a place difficult to access. Here, the mothers ran the home and educated their children.

2 **THE *ANDRON***
An area exclusive to men, the *andron* was where visitors were received, and feasts and symposia were held. Delicacies were placed in front of each guest on stools.

3 **IDEAS OF HYGIENE**
Personal cleanliness was very important to the Greeks. There were washing rooms in the houses, with stone or brick bathtubs. These were filled with water from a well, and then patiently emptied by hand.

SOLE ENTRANCE
Entry was made through a wooden door that had a lock. This led into the open central patio.

4 **INSIDE COURTYARD**
Rooms were laid out around a central patio, which provided light and air. In this open space, which was for the entire family, an altar for sacrifices to the family gods occupied a prominent position.

Restrictions

In the Greek world, there was a well-known distinction between the public sphere and the private or domestic sphere. The former was reserved for commerce and male politics, and the latter for the development of the family, considered the basic nucleus of society. The links between their members were limited. Theater entertainment was one of the few instances where all members of a family could share in a common activity. At the same time, these events reflected the inequality that existed between the sexes and the different social sectors. For example, women were prohibited from acting, and poor people occupied the stands that were farthest away from the stage.

Choice of Spouse

Marriage between Greeks was based on convenience instead of sentiment. A period of engagement was compulsory before the consummation of any marriage. The bride was handed over to the bridegroom by her closest male relative. If this ceremony failed to take place, the marriage could be declared null. The time between the engagement and the marriage itself was filled with various religious celebrations. On these occasions, women of all ages from the families concerned had a unique opportunity to participate at festivities. The celebrations started early in the bride's house, and at dusk the woman was escorted in a bridal carriage to the groom's residence. It was normal for young women to get married at fifteen years of age, with their husbands being older. Moreover, the bride and groom did not meet each other until the very moment of the wedding. The majority of wedding engagements occurred at a time of year called *Gamelion*, the month of the Greek calendar that corresponds to our January and February.

Unions Ruled by Men

Marriage was a contract that constrained only the women; men could reject them, have concubines, and keep the children after divorce. The city of Athens invented democracy. However, its laws were very different to those of today. The only people with full rights were free men.

FROM HAND TO HAND

Legitimate wives had to be daughters of citizens. When women got married, they changed guardians, with authority passing from their father to their husband. They did not have individual rights.

Family Recreation Outside the Home

Males held ultimate authority within the home and outside it. All family members agreed to decisions made by the father within the private and public spheres. One of the few family outings occurred during the *Dionysia*—festivities in honor of the god Dionysus, at which plays were performed.

1 **ACTORS AND PLAYS**
Actors were single men, who mostly formed the chorus, which related and interpreted the different stories. The plays could be tragedies or comedies.

3 **THE AUDIENCE**
People from other city-states attended the theater in Athens. Unless you were a magistrate with his place reserved, it was difficult to find a seat.

2 **SEATS OF PRIVILEGE**
Distinguished local politicians were always situated in the first rows, while their families sat behind them. Access to the theater was unrestricted and free.

4 **PUBLIC APPROVAL**
The audience showed their approval or disapproval of a play by means of applause.

LIFE IN THE OPEN AIR
Public life was a male activity. Women had very few opportunities to go out of their homes. They were allowed to attend religious celebrations and plays, which were well attended.

FEMALE ROLES
Greek women were not permitted to act. If a play required female characters, they were represented by men who covered their faces with masks and wore shoes with high heels.

The Taste of Olives

From antiquity, Greece functioned as a nexus between the Western world and the Far East, and managed to establish culinary traditions that are still in use today. Olives, wheat, and wine represent the basic trilogy in Mediterranean cooking traditions. The oldest Greek records about olive growing come from the island of Crete and date from approximately 2500 BC. In the Homeric poems olive oil is called "liquid gold," emphasizing the importance that it had for customs of the age. In Greek mythology, it is believed that the goddess Athena gained the patronage of Athens after showing her people the multiple benefits of growing olives.

The Three Meals of the Day

The Greeks were accustomed to having three meals a day. Some time just before dawn, they had *acratismos*, or breakfast: some pieces of wheat or barley bread were soaked in a little pure wine. On occasions, they added generous portions of olives or figs. Midday was the time for *ariston*, a quick dinner that was light and cold and could include bread, olives, cereals, and fruit. The most substantial meal was the *deipnon*, or dinner, with a dessert consisting of fresh or dry fruit, especially figs, nuts, grapes, and honey. All solid food eaten with bread was called *opson*, a relish—be it vegetables, olives, fish, or fruit. People connected to the army ate a lot of garlic, cheese, and onions, because these foods were thought to be good omens.

DECANTING
Oil was separated from impurities and water in amphorae.

OLIVE PASTE
One or two men would push the wheel to process the olives to make a paste.

LIQUID GOLD

Olives were the main crop in ancient Greece. They were not only used in cooking but also as a cosmetic, an essence, a tribute to the gods and sportsmen, and as a fuel for night lights, among other things. In particular, the use of olive oil marked a form of regional cuisine that is now called "Mediterranean," and which comprises a group of culinary styles from the southern Mediterranean countries.

OLIVE PICKING
The fruits were collected one by one.

ON TIME
The olives were gathered when they reached the correct level of maturity.

1 HARVESTING
The branches were shaken with sticks so that the mature olives would fall into blankets lying on the ground.

2 MILLING
The olives were put into the mill whole, and ground by large stones to create a special thick paste.

3 PRESSING
Circular baskets made of natural fibers were filled with olive paste. Then, by applying pressure, the oil was extracted.

Costly Production

The olive was the most widespread fruit crop, but processing the oil required a great deal of effort. This was because the oil content in the pulp could fluctuate between 17 percent and 30 percent, depending on the variety.

CLASSIFICATION
Olives were separated, either to be used for oil or for table consumption.

EXTRACTING OIL
Heavy rocks were hung from a press so that oil could be extracted.

Classical Training

In fifth-century BC Athens, a group of institutions and educational practices was established based on the wealth created by the work of slaves, and attuned to the economic and cultural splendor of the city. The Athenians invented the first democratic system. This was based on assemblies, at which all citizens—free adult males born in the city—could participate. Consequently, they would be trained in an education system that spanned infancy to adulthood. Within this context, the teaching of philosophy was consolidated and Socrates, Plato, and Aristotle started to develop the subject in open spaces.

Paideia

The *paideia*, the model used for training the Athenian citizen, consisted of literary, artistic, and physical teaching. From about seven years of age, the boys of citizens attended the "schools" in the schoolmaster's house accompanied by the educator, a slave assigned to that purpose. Between the ages of twelve and fourteen, they started their sports and artistic training. At eighteen, they were declared to be *ephebes*, with the state at this point concerning itself with their military, political, and administrative education for a period of three years. At twenty-one, they were considered to be citizens with full legal rights. Many then went to classes with the Sophists—free teachers who taught the disciplines needed for participation in the assembly, such as rhetoric, eloquence, and argument. Some citizens attended philosophy schools, such as Plato's Academy and Aristotle's Lyceum. It was here that pedagogy was recognized as a branch of knowledge with a certain autonomy from other philosophical and religious subjects. There were also schools for craftsmen held in workshops, while free women learned reading and a little arithmetic in their classes.

First Writing

The teacher taught individual classes in his house. A stylus was used for writing, and sacred literary works, written on rolls of parchment, were used for reading.

Instructing the Democrat

Pericles (495 BC–429 BC) was an important Athenian governor and military strategist. He supported various measures in the assembly to improve and strengthen the democratic model, which promoted education for citizens.

THE ARENAS

Arenas were the spaces devoted to sports training for young people. They were generally associated with a gymnasium.

MUSIC SCHOOL

For Athenians, artistic training was considered just as necessary as intellectual or physical training.

Plato's Academy

This school of philosophy—understood as the sum of all knowledge—was founded by Plato around 388 BC in the gardens of the Academy. This was situated in an olive grove on the outskirts of Athens, and was dedicated to the goddess Athena.

1 EXCLUSIVE SITE
This was an open venue on whose facade Plato expressed the following: "Let no one enter here who does not know mathematics."

2 EDUCATOR
The teacher gave his classes orally, while walking, by means of a question-and-answer system.

3 PUPILS
Male citizens with available time attended Plato's Academy of their own free will.

ACADEMOS
The Academy owes its name to the legendary hero Academos.

END OF THE ACADEMY

In the sixth century AD, the emperor Justinian I banned classes of Greek philosophy.

Great Masters

In order to cover all fields of knowledge, Plato invited learned men, such as mathematicians, astronomers, and doctors of medicine, to teach classes.

War and Obedience

Sparta was a Greek state based on rigid military organization, in which its members were brought up as soldiers to serve their country and give their lives for it. The army and its conquests determined everything that was done. Profitable activities were carried out by the *Perioikoi* (inhabitants from the outskirts without political rights) and *Helots* (servants belonging to the Spartan state). The great goal of the *Spartiates*, the dominant class, was to train themselves for war and the honor of their land. Although a minority, they led the army and held public positions. For that purpose, they were raised from childhood in rigor, heroism, and obedience.

The *Agoge*

All children were examined at birth by a committee of elders, because they were considered to belong to the state and not to their parents. If they were healthy and well formed, they could be admitted into the city. Otherwise they were thrown from Mount Taygetus. The aim was to prevent the patriotic warrior race from weakening. Healthy boys were sent to a farm worked by helots on the outskirts of the city. They had to live on that farm's income until they died, when it would be handed over to another child. Young children became accustomed to being alone, and they were encouraged to become strong, not to fear the dark, to get dirty, to climb trees, to scale rocks, to hurt themselves, to bear pain and punishment, and to walk naked to toughen the skin. Whims or tantrums were forbidden, and they had to remain silent as much as possible. At seven years of age, boys had to enter state-run institutions, where they received the specific military training required to confirm their role as Spartan warriors.

Sporting Skill

Spartan fighters were outstanding at sports. Their athletes won many victories in competitions, such as the Olympic Games.

A FEATURE OF ADULTHOOD
At fifteen years of age boys, were allowed to grow their hair. Long hair was characteristic of soldiers.

1

THE *AGELAI*
On entry to military training, boys were shaved and placed in an *agelai*, or herd, according to their age.

Education of Women

In contrast to other young Greek women, Spartan girls received an education that was physically demanding, so that they would be able to have strong and healthy offspring. Here are Spartan girls as painted by Degas (left) and Corot (right).

Soldier Training

At around seven years old, boys entered the gymnasiums, where they remained under the command of a *paedonomo*—a magistrate who supervised their education—and they were instructed by a young man called an *eiren*. From about twelve years of age, physical exercise became more important, and they were taught how to handle a lance and shield, and how to form a phalanx—a formation used in battle.

1 IN CHARGE
The *eiren* gave out orders, taught combat tactics, and trained the little children. Only young men could become *eirens*, and when at least eighteen years old, which was the age of maturity.

2 GAMES
To encourage competition, violence, and teamwork, boys played a ball game that was similar to rugby but more brutal and with fewer rules. The players were called *sfareis*.

3 UNDER STATE TUTELAGE
During the learning process, children and young people were excluded from citizenship. All links with their families were lost and they depended directly on the state.

4 PUNISHMENTS
It was normal for one child to hit another with a bamboo stick. Those being punished became used to bearing the pain, while those doing the hitting "learned" not to hesitate in their attack.

Lycurgus

The creation of Spartan law was attributed to the mythical legislator Lycurgus, as was the constitution known as the *Rhetra*, which governed city life. It is believed that he also conceived the *agoge*, although there is no historic evidence for this.

FIGHTING AND ATHLETICISM
Athletic and military activities, including arms handling, were carried out in the open air.

EVERYTHING FOR SPARTA
Spartans were seeking to instill self-confidence in the boys, as well as total respect for their superiors and absolute loyalty to Sparta.

Rival States

Spartan armies, educated in the *agoge*, conquered Laconia and annexed Mesenia. The pastoral people from Arcadia, portrayed here by Poussin, were some of the few that resisted their hegemony.

First Performances

Emerging in Athens in response to religious celebrations honoring the god Dionysus, Greek theater emerged about the sixth century BC, and provided a foundation for theater in the West. The works of the classical masters of tragedy (Aeschylus, Sophocles, and Euripides) and of comedy (Aristophanes) were the forerunners of modern theatrical performances. At the start, the chorus had a central role in the unfolding of events, the works included song and dance, a maximum of three actors were allowed per scene, and women were not allowed to act. In spite of these differences compared to today's theater, all the later playwrights, from Seneca to Shakespeare and Molière, from O'Neill to Pirandello, from Brecht to Bernard Shaw, were much indebted to these old masters.

Created for Seeing

The word "theater" comes from the Greek *théatron*—"place for seeing"—and was originally applied to that part of the amphitheater assigned to the public. Eventually, it was applied to the whole building, as well as to the genre itself. The theater recognizes its origins in the *dithyramb*, a poetic form sung by the chorus and celebrated at festivals in honor of the god Dionysus. According to Greek tradition, the first playwright—also the first actor—was Thespis, who, in the middle of the sixth century BC, in Athens, separated himself from the chorus as a soloist, but interacted with the *coryphaeus* (leader of the chorus). Later, in the fifth century BC, Aeschylus introduced a second actor onto the stage, at the same time reducing the chorus of fifty people to twelve. His contemporary, Sophocles (author of *Oedipus Rex*), added a third actor. Euripides, the third great Greek tragedian, deepened the psychological makeup of the characters, and, at the same time, frequently used the *deus ex machina* resource, toward the end of the play—the interruption of a god, who resolved the conflict that developed in the course of the tragedy.

CHORUS
As time passed, the role of the chorus, who commented on the action on the stage, diminished.

THEATER WITH MASKS
The actors used masks that represented certain established characters. This, given the great size of the amphitheaters, allowed the action to be followed more easily, at the same time as making the female characters more realistic.

ORCHESTRA
The chorus sang and performed its dances in the *orchestra*.

The Structure of the Theater

The area where the plays were performed was divided into three parts: the *orchestra*, a circular space, was where the action took place; behind this was the *skené*, which framed the action; while the semicircular *auditorium*, which surrounded the orchestra, was where the audience was situated.

MACHINERY
The gods entered the story line by means of a type of crane.

GODS
A god often intervened to resolve the plot.

Greek Influence

Theater appeared in Rome toward the third century BC and was a direct legacy of the Greek tradition. The most outstanding playwrights from this period were the comedians Plautus and Terence (second century BC) and Seneca (first century AD), author of tragedies.

SCENERY
The panels of the *skené* gave context to the scenes.

DRESSING ROOM
The actor changed in the *skené*, for later scenes.

1 PROTAGONIST
In early theater, there was only one actor. In later plays, there were up to three actors per scene.

2 FEMALE ROLES
Women were forbidden to act; their place was taken by disguised men.

Competing for Glory

The Olympic Games were part of a religious celebration in honor of Zeus, the "father of the gods." The first Games took place in the Olympic sanctuary in the year 776 BC, and were held for more than eleven centuries, until Christian Rome banned them at the end of the fourth century AD. They took place every four years (always in Olympia) and were the most important athletic festival in Greece. In times of war, competitors were able to travel, unhindered, in order to attend the Games. The winners achieved fame throughout Greece, and were considered heroes. As well as sports, there were animal sacrifices and displays from sculptors and poets.

Sporting Festival

There were four athletic competitions in ancient Greece called the Panhellenic Games: the Nemean Games, Isthmian Games, Pythian Games, and the Olympic Games. The last event was the most famous (so much so that years were counted in Olympiads, the space of four years between one Games and the next). At first, they lasted for only one day and consisted of only one competition: the *stadion*—a running race of about 210 yards (190 meters). Later, they added other events, and the length of the Games was established as five days (the last dedicated to awarding prizes). Some of the typical events were boxing, chariot racing, and racing with armor, but there were no competitions for team or ball games. Although there were competitions for women in other festivals, the Games were reserved for men, and only for those belonging to Greek culture. According to some historical records, women were even forbidden to attend as spectators.

Triumphal Entrance

The entrance arch to the *stadion* is the oldest and most reputable evidence of the Olympic Games.

The Great Victory

The goddess Nike (Victory) symbolized the glory and athletic excellence of the Olympic Games winners. This statue (left) is the *Winged Victory of Samothrace*, which is now in the Louvre in Paris.

DISCIPLINES

Some events are still practiced in the modern Games, such as the long jump and throwing the javelin and discus (left).

Olympic Sanctuary

The sanctuary was under the control of the city-state of Elis. Here, the Temple of Hera and the Temple of Zeus stood out. In the latter was found the famous Olympic statue of Zeus, one of the wonders of the ancient world. The race courses for runners and chariots were situated to the east. To the west was the building for the athletes' accommodation and the arena—a practice space for the fighters.

Crown of Laurel

In most Games, it was normal to compete naked; this was not considered scandalous. In the Temple of Zeus, the winners' only prize was a laurel wreath and public admiration.

1 **PRYTANEION**
Situated beside the Temple of Hera, this was where the priests and magistrates lived.

2 **TEMPLE OF ZEUS**
Inside the temple was the Olympian Zeus statue, made by Phidias (architect of the Parthenon).

3 **STADIUM**
The running races took place in the stadium. The chariot race circuit was around the edge of the stadium.

TREASURES
The buildings situated at the foot of Mount Kronos harbored offerings.

PUBLIC
The event attracted huge crowds from the whole of Greece.

DISTINGUISHED VISITORS
Special guests were lodged in pavilions situated around the Temple of Zeus.

Free Thinkers

The ancient Greeks are remembered for their philosophical thought and debate. Philosophers started as scholars who devoted themselves to searching for truth by definition. These restless thinkers were not content with the answers hitherto provided by religion and, as a consequence, they were focused on discovering the origin of all things, assigning themselves the task of promoting investigation into natural phenomena. They were not satisfied with the explanations given by traditional myths, but looked to rational explanation for the questions under consideration. The ancient Greek philosophers tried hard to understand the world around them and, of course, their own existence.

Love of Wisdom

Philosophers emerged in the School of Miletus, in Asia Minor, in the sixth century BC. Because of their critical analysis of reality, on many occasions they made enemies of the political and religious authorities in ancient Greece. The creation of the word *philosophy*, a Greek concept that means "love of wisdom," is usually attributed to Pythagoras of Samos. The first intellectuals observed that nature was ruled by established laws, and they tried to discover the primordial element from which the universe had arisen. In the fifth century BC, philosophical speculation centered on the study of humankind. A group of educators appeared, known as Sophists, who charged high fees for their classes and denied the existence of an absolute truth. Socrates was their fervent opponent; he believed in the existence of a universal truth possessed by each man, which could be brought out from under the surface through education.

1 EPICURUS
The philosopher Epicurus supported the view that human pleasure was the absence of pain, and he understood life in terms of chance.

2 DIOGENES
Living as a tramp in Athens, Diogenes transformed extreme poverty into the virtue of knowledge.

3 ANAXIMANDER
By means of a process of pure observation, Anaximander concluded that life must have started in water.

4 PARMENIDES
Parmenides believed that fire had been the start of everything. He declared, "to be and to think are the same."

BEYOND GREECE

To analyze, or philosophize about, society is a distinguishing feature of the human condition. Since antiquity, different thinkers have contributed to the understanding of the world that surrounded them, and at the same time have become "voices" of the social processes they were living through.

**500 BC
CONFUCIUS**
At fifty years of age, Confucius (left) started his teachings, based on good conduct in life, just government, tradition, and meditation.

**1195
AVERROES**
Averroes (left) was exiled from Al-Andalus because of his "double truth theory," which suggests arriving at universal knowledge by way of faith or reason.

From the East: Philosophy And Beliefs

TAOISM

Lao-Tse is one of the most relevant philosophers among Chinese intellectuals. He emphasized the "Tao" and the "Way," understood in terms of respect for the way in which things naturally grow and decline.

BUDDHISM

Siddharta Guatama is a sacred figure who expressed the mystical idea that the route to inner peace involves an enormous sacrifice, and it usually starts with a provocative and disturbing doubt.

Philosophers in Art

The Athens School is one of the most famous works created by the Renaissance artist Raffaello Sanzio. Philosophy is represented here by an imaginary session between the principal thinkers of classical antiquity. Plato and his disciple Aristotle are shown debating the topic of the search for truth, making gestures that correspond to their theoretical conceptions: the first points to the sky, while the second points to the earth. Socrates, father of critical philosophy and Plato's master, is represented in profile.

5 PTOLEMY
Devoted to astronomy, Ptolemy was the author of the geocentric organization model, with the earth as the center of the universe. This was supported by the Catholic Church during the Middle Ages.

6 PLOTINUS
The thinking of Plotinus is interpreted as a "system," the system of One, which embraces and considers totality as a whole ruled by the metaphysical law of unity.

7 PLATO
Plato wrote about politics and the existence of two worlds: the real and the ideal.

8 ARISTOTLE
Possessing an encyclopedic knowledge, Aristotle systematized all the sciences.

9 SOCRATES
Socrates maintained the principle that without analysis life is not worth living.

1252
SAINT THOMAS OF AQUINAS
At the start of his teaching career, he stood out for the clarity of his explanations, a methodical articulation of concepts and influence in Catholicism.

1637
RENÉ DESCARTES
In his work *Discourse on Method*, he suggested his maxim: "I think therefore I am," which breaks with scholastic tradition and establishes the basis of modern philosophy.

1897
FRIEDRICH NIETZSCHE
Nietzsche developed the idea of multiple perspectives as a way of challenging the reader to consider various facets of the same topic.

1929
JEAN-PAUL SARTRE
Sartre (left) married his colleague and companion Simone de Beauvoir. With his wife and Albert Camus, he helped define existentialism. He viewed freedom as a both a liberation and a burden.

Owners of the Mediterranean

The first people of antiquity to practice commerce on a grand scale were the Phoenicians. Originating from what is today the Lebanon coast, for centuries they were masters of the whole Mediterranean. They took their products to all the coasts and exchanged them for local merchandise, sometimes trading with important cities or nations. The Phoenicians established great commercial colonies throughout the region. One such colony became the cradle of another great civilization: Carthage.

The Port of Carthage

Founded in northern Africa in the ninth century BC, Carthage rivaled Rome until its destruction in the second century BC.

WOOD
The Phoenicians generally used Lebanese cedar for their construction work.

TRADERS
The most prosperous merchants could be found in the upper echelons of Phoenician society; moreover, they usually held government posts.

EXPORTS
Manufactured goods were loaded in Carthage. These included dyed textiles and bronze objects, as well as ceramics and glass.

IMPORTS
Garo (a kind of lobster), metals such as tin and gold, slaves, marble, and purple dyes arrived at Carthage from all over the Mediterranean.

Eclectic Art

Phoenician art consisted of a mixture of styles and is difficult to define. It incorporated Egyptian, Greek, Mesopotamian, Aegean, and Syrian elements, among others.

A Magical Dye

Why does a civilization suddenly stand out from the rest? Answering this question is not easy. We know that the Phoenicians had several things in their favor. On the one hand, they lived on coasts that were suitable for establishing natural ports. Their forests were abundant with wood—ideal for constructing vessels. Next, they produced a range of products made from ceramic and glass, and textiles colored with a dye called Tyrian purple, which they obtained from a mollusk and was particularly valued in the Mediterranean. The Romans were wildly enthusiastic about garments dyed with Phoenician purple, and about the color itself, because, in contrast to other colors, it did not fade over time. Toward the sixth century BC, commercial rivalry with the Greeks drifted into military conflict, in which the Phoenicians would be defeated.

TOWARD THE SEA
It is possible that one of the main factors that pushed the Phoenicians toward the sea was the soil and the climate where they lived, which were not particularly suited to agriculture.

WINE
The Phoenicians introduced and distributed wine and winemaking across large parts of the Mediterranean.

GALLEYS
Phoenician galleys were called *biremes* or *triremes*. These had one large sail that was used when the wind was behind. Big, rounded ships could, however, take greater quantities of cargo.

Ancient Rome

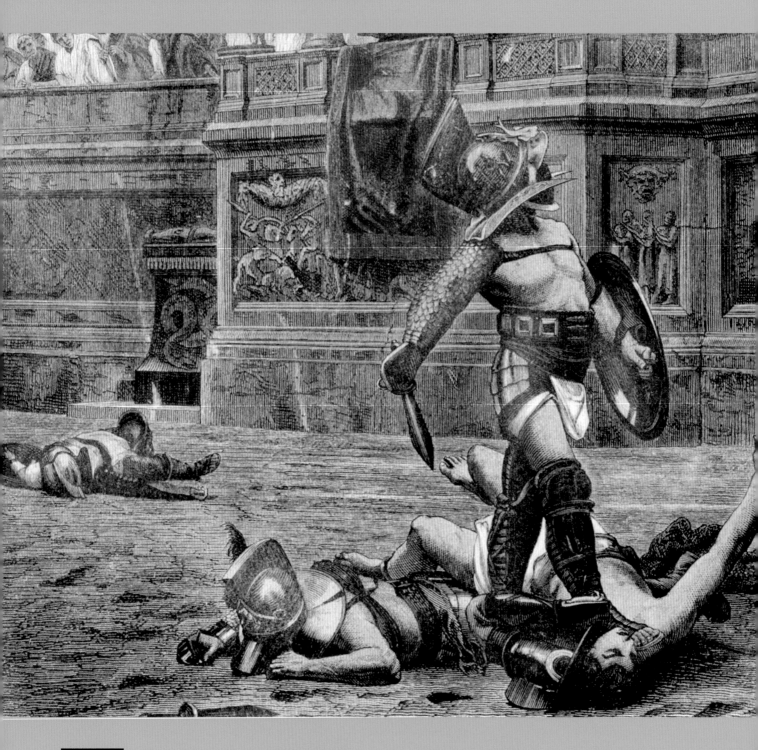

The history of ancient Rome is usually divided into three main periods: before the rise of Rome; the Roman Republic; and the Roman Empire, which lasted for more than seven centuries. The first inhabitants of the area that became Rome were farmers who settled on the Palatine Hill

in about 1000 BC. In 500 BC, Rome became a republic and began to flex its muscles with the conquest of Italy. The population of Rome had reached one million by 50 BC, one year before Julius Caesar crossed the Rubicon to become dictator and give rise to the age of the all-powerful emperors who ruled over the vast Roman Empire.

Buildings for the People

During the time of the empire, the Roman population increased. What had started as a small community became a large, populous city, and the lack of dwellings became a major problem. To overcome this housing shortage, *insulae* appeared; these were multifamily constructions—the antecedents of more modern buildings. Each *insula* occupied one block and contained a large number of apartments in different sizes. While a rich family would live in a spacious *domus*, the poorer sectors of the population could only rent small, less comfortable spaces in these domestic buildings.

The Insula

The term *insula* comes from the word for "island." These buildings were so called because each one took up an entire block, surrounded by streets or spaces that had not been built on. The housing needs of a growing population led Roman architects to design these early buildings, usually on five floors, providing apartments with several rooms and also studios.

CONSTRUCTION MATERIAL

The first *insulae* were built with wood and clay, because they were the cheapest materials. However, due to the fact that structures would often collapse, and because of the risk of fire, the use of bricks and concrete became more common over time.

The Domus

The marked social differences in Roman society were reflected in their dwellings. The *domus* were luxurious and comfortable residences with multiple rooms occupied by the most powerful families. They were organized around an axis, from the hall to the *peristyle*. In the center was the *atrium*, the heart of the home. There were spaces reserved for visitors, and others for the exclusive use of the household.

STORES

Commercial premises and bars were situated on the ground floor of the building. Sellers displayed the products most closely associated with their trade.

DANGER
The *insulae* were in a very precarious condition. Regular fires and structural collapses led to the emergence of fire teams and the establishment of safety measures, including limitations on the number of floors.

RENTING
Powerful Romans invested in the building of *insulae* and then rented out apartments at a fairly high cost.

AMBITUS
The *ambitus* was the name of the free space between one *insula* and another. The imperial regulations demanded that this space should be about 3 feet (1 meter) wide.

HEIGHT AND STATUS
The apartments on the first floor were bigger and more expensive than those above, which were accessed by narrow and winding wooden stairs.

1 **WITHOUT A KITCHEN OR BATHROOM**
The rooms did not have a distinct function. Any room could be used for eating or sleeping; there were no toilet facilities and cooking was done on a brazier.

2 **WINDOWS AND BALCONIES**
These openings, the only source of ventilation and light, were small and were protected with wooden shutters. Some apartments had external balconies.

3 **THROWN ONTO THE STREET**
The piles of garbage and filth were constant. Human waste and debris were stored in containers, eventually to be flung out of the windows.

Gens and Paterfamilias

The city of Rome was formed from an association of groups of people that recognized themselves as descendants of a common ancestor. Each of these groups or families constituted a *gens,* or clan, and their members were called patricians. The word "patrician" derives from the Latin *patres,* which refers to the leaders or fathers of the *gens*. In their origins, they consisted of a closed group that monopolized all political, economic, and religious power. Many people who did not belong to any clan put themselves under the protection of a patrician *paterfamilias* and were referred to as clients. The families were large and extended, because the married couple, their children, and other close relatives all lived together in the same household.

The *Patria Potestas*

The Roman extended family consisted of a group of three or more generations who lived in one residence or in dwellings very close by. For example, grandparents, brothers and their wives, uncles, aunts, nephews, and nieces could all live together. Each family depended on the overall authority of a father or *paterfamilias* (head of the family), who was represented by the oldest male in the home. Only one man could exercise this authority at any one time. Even adult children continued to live under the father's authority and could not acquire the rights of the *paterfamilias* while their father was still living. The power of the *paterfamilias* was absolute and for life and included the *potestas,* or jurisdiction, over the group of family members. This meant that when children were born, they were left at the feet of the father. If the father accepted the child, he lifted it in his arms. If he did not, the babies were "exposed"—they were left on the public thoroughfare to die, or until a compassionate person or someone in need of children picked them up. Similarly, the *paterfamilias* had the power to authorize or reject his children's marriages, because when a woman married, she and her possessions passed into the control of her husband.

1. **PATERFAMILIAS**
The *paterfamilias* was the head of the family, and everyone lived under his authority; clients and slaves owed him absolute respect.

2. **WOMEN**
Although they were subject to the law, women depended on the *paterfamilias*. This applied to mothers and sisters, as well as daughters.

3. **DOMESTIC FAMILY**
Based on blood relationships, the *paterfamilias* had everyone at his disposal, as though they were his property. His word was law.

Roman Marriage

Marriage had to be between people of the same social strata: patrician men with patrician women, plebeian men with plebeian women—the latter being commoners, who did not belong to a clan. The marriage rites included the use of rings, a wedding kiss, the joining of hands, the bride's veil, and the parents' consent.

MEMORABLE TWINS

According to legend, when the twins Romulus and Remus, the founders of Rome, were young, they were nursed by a wolf. They were children of the god Mars and Rhea Silvia, a princess, who was also related by marriage to the Greek goddess Aphrodite.

4 CLIENT FAMILY
The client family was made up of people who lacked blood ties or kinship with the *paterfamilias*, but who depended on his ultimate will and authority. It was regulated by political, economic, and religious ties.

5 CHILDREN
Education was centered on the family and the father established the guidelines, which could not be questioned. The ideal was to cultivate manliness and self-control in boys and obedience in girls. Powerful families had slave educators.

PUBLIC LIFE
Men and women from all social sectors moved around and lived together in the busy streets of the city of Rome. Even slaves could walk about freely to do the shopping.

More than a Home

The *domus* was the name given to a patrician's residence in ancient Rome. It was not just a dwelling. It was here that political meetings took place, as well as commercial transactions, social gatherings, and private religious ceremonies. The *paterfamilias*, or head of the family, was the person who wielded absolute domestic power as head of the *domus*. According to tradition, he held four *potestas*, or basic powers, over his wife, children, clients, and slaves. The *atrium*, or central courtyard, was the only place used by all the people living in the residence. The remaining rooms had specific uses, in particular, the *tablinum*, or office, of the *paterfamilias*.

Heart of the Home

The arrangement of the *domus* reflected the familial and social organization of the ancient Romans. A traditional residence was built around an *atrium*, the heart of the home. Business meetings were held, and visitors were also received, in this space. For this reason, the *paterfamilias* took great care over how it was decorated and he contracted well-known artists to create frescoes and sculptures. In the atrium was the *compluvium* (a high opening through which rainwater entered), together with the *impluvium* (a small central tank that was linked to a subterranean cistern). Any member of the family or servant could access this area, although they could not enter the *tablinum*.

DECORATION

The rooms were built around courtyards. The inside walls were decorated with painted scenes.

UNIONS

Roman women usually got married young to older men. The minimum age was twelve years old for women and fourteen years old for men. Marriages were arranged by the parents of the bride and groom.

DOMESTIC CULT

Religious worship in the home included praise for the souls of the *lares*, or ancestors. When they were beneficent, they were called *manes*, and if they were wrongdoers, *larvae*. The *paterfamilias* offered libations among the *penates*, which were statuettes that represented the protecting spirits of the home. Each home honored particular hearths with special dedication, care, and respect. It was an intimate place.

Family and Business at Home

The Roman *domus* was the center of important family, political, and economic relationships. At all hours, relatives and businessmen were moving around, as were slaves who were obeying orders or who needed the *paterfamilias* to make some decision.

1 PATERFAMILIAS
As well as all the powers he held, the *paterfamilias* was the only owner of the family patrimony and the head of the domestic cult of *sacra privata*. Everyone paid him complete respect.

Attendants

Patrician women did not do any work with their hands. They were assisted by slaves at all times: while getting washed, when they left the house, and in caring for their children.

2 MATRONA
The word *matrona* derives from the Latin *mater*: it was given to a woman who was married to a patrician man.

3 THE LIFE OF A SLAVE
The philosopher Seneca said: "Treat your slave with kindness." However, slaves were considered to be objects. Cleaning and cooking were among their responsibilities.

4 LARARIUM
In a corner of the atrium was the *lararium*, a niche devoted to the domestic cult. Of great significance, it guarded statuettes of the ancestors.

5 CLIENTELE
This was mainly composed of impoverished plebeians, who offered their services to the *paterfamilias* and remained under his command for all kinds of activities.

6 BRINGING UP CHILDREN
In ancient Rome, there was no free education. Many powerful families contracted teachers who specialized in oration to educate their children.

KITCHEN
This was an environment of constant activity, and the place in which food was prepared.

FOOD
Most food was basic, and included *pulmentum*, or millet gruel, barley, and goat cheese.

Drink of the Gods

From antiquity, wine was used as an offering to the gods in Mediterranean cultures. The Romans adopted this religious tradition from their neighbors, the Greeks, and it spread throughout Western Europe. They devoted special care to the gratification of the gods Vesta and Bacchus, with libations in their homes and temples. Moreover, they introduced technical innovations to the cultivation of the vine. These are still used in modern winemaking processes; for example, consideration of the climate and orography (mountain geography) when choosing the variety of grape to plant, the effects of pruning on yield and wine quality, maturing the wine after fermentation, and the importance of cleanliness in the process.

Wine for All

The Roman conquests produced extraordinary revenues, and the patricians invested in impressive *villas*, or agricultural settlements, in every corner of the empire. Wine became popular for daily consumption and for offerings to the gods, and as a result the whole of Lazio became filled with vineyards. The emperor Domitian even had to forbid the plantation of new stock so that there would not be a scarcity of cereals. The area with the best vineyards was Pompeii, but after its destruction in AD 79, the Romans had to import wine from plantations in Gaul and the Iberian Peninsula. The cult of Bacchus, god of wine, was widespread. The Romans developed the orgiastic and recreational components of the Bacchanalia, a festival in which, by consuming excessive amounts of alcohol, they could make contact with the god. The goddess Vesta, principal divinity of the patricians, represented the soul of the home and family. She received wine and food in her temple on the Roman Forum, which was presided over by the Vestal Virgins.

Traditional Labor

The Roman plantations had immense structures for treading grapes and extracting the must—juices that contain various things, such as peel and seeds. White and black grapes were separated in the production of a variety of wines.

EQUIPMENT
Treading of the grapes required the strength of a group of slaves.

1

GRAPE JUICE
It was believed that grape juice or "must" had very beneficial medicinal properties.

The Roman Grape Harvest

The production of Roman wine included the treading of the grapes shortly after harvesting. The grape juice was stored in a large, half-buried earthenware container called a *dolium*, in which fermentation would take place. Later, the wine was taken out and stored in *amphorae* for distribution. Sweet white wine was the most appreciated in the Roman world, and its alcohol was often diluted with water.

 LAGAR
This was the name of the space where the concrete vessels for treading the grapes were found: a winepress. The grape juice was spilt through the central channel.

 DOLIA
These large earthenware or ceramic containers were kept buried and covered up in order to encourage fermentation. They held hundreds of gallons.

Wineries

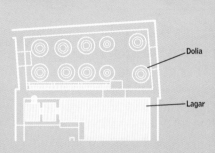

Dolia

Lagar

The countryside villas, assigned to grape cultivation, had facilities for making wine. This diagram shows the prototype of a winery in Pompeii.

AMINEAN
The best class of grape in the empire was called *aminean*.

CAPACITY
Depending on size, each container could store 53 to 530 gallons (200 to 2,000 liters).

MUSLUM
Wine with honey and aromatic herbs, known as *muslum*, was served at banquets.

FERMENTATION
This lasted around thirty days, and then the wine would be poured into large earthenware jars.

The Might of Rome

The Roman Empire was in its heyday around the first century AD, after conquering the whole of the Mediterranean and then advancing into more distant regions, including Great Britain and Mesopotamia in Asia. Its language was imposed as a universal means of communication and was used for administrative purposes implemented via an extensive network of roads, which united the different parts of the vast empire. Heirs to the Greek culture, the Romans borrowed some of its elements, such as its educational practices, although they took a more realistic and pragmatic approach. Thus, for example, the study of law and engineering ranked above that of philosophy and thought.

A Public Matter

The Roman Empire considered education to be a public issue. Citizens created a group of municipal schools, supported and supervised by the state. They also established official chairs of rhetoric, Greek language, and philosophy, with teachers paid by the *aerarium* (treasury). Boys learned to read and write at seven years of age, taught either in private homes or in municipal schools. Thereafter, some pupils between twelve and sixteen years of age went on to grammar school, which provided the teaching of Greek and Latin grammar, the reading of the classics, and the study of rhetoric and oratory. Lessons were given in Greek, because most of the students were of Greek origin, as well as in Latin. Finally, for the governing minority, there was the school of rhetoric; this included philosophy lessons and was directed toward teaching law.

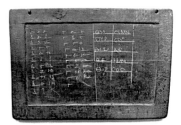

Wax Tablets

Writing was learned by making marks with a pointed tool or stylus on wax tablets that could be reused.

TRAINING
Weapons of wood, cane, and other less dangerous materials were used for practice.

Social Distinction

In Imperial Rome, there were many different educational practices. These varied according to which social strata they were aimed at and depended on the social status and duties that were required of each particular group.

1 LITERACY
Pupils were taught in schools from the age of seven.

2 GLADIATOR SCHOOLS
Future gladiators received strict training so as to participate in circus games—the main Roman spectacle.

3 REGULATED PRACTICES
The *lanistas*, or old gladiators, taught the rules of combat to the new practitioners.

4 TEACHER
The teacher dressed in splendid clothes and wore a moustache and beard so that his importance and rank would stand out.

5 ROMAN FORUM
The center of political, economic, and cultural life of the city, parts of the forum were also set aside for education.

6 RHETORIC CLASSES
"Speaking well" or rhetoric was taught for performance in public spaces, such as the Senate.

7 MEN OF LETTERS
Inherited from the Greeks, rhetoric was a subject of study by thinkers and politicians, such as Cicero.

The Vestal Virgins

Priestesses known as the Vestal Virgins were elected and trained to take care of the sacred fire of the goddess Vesta, and to carry out their respective rituals.

The First Great Amphitheater

There were more than 250 amphitheaters in the Roman Empire, but the biggest and most famous was the Colosseum, whose original name was the Flavian Amphitheater. It was built between the years AD 70 and AD 80 by the emperor Vespasian and his son and successor, Titus. With its oval shape, it could seat 50,000 spectators, who would enter through one of the seventy-six entrances (another four were reserved for the emperor and distinguished people). Gladiatorial contests were held there, as well as fights against animals, mock battles, and mythological scene reenactments.

Combats and Huge Crowds

Historians of the period, such as Suetonius and Cassius Dio, witnessed bloody performances of naval combat held at the Colosseum, with the arena being flooded by means of a system of canals. Those spectacles could not continue when the subterranean galleries (*hypogea*) were built, which allowed animals to come onto the stage. The scale of this new work meant that careful planning was essential. Keeping the Colosseum functioning required the labor and coordination of hundreds of people; the crowds at these spectacles were huge.

250 POLES
With ropes, these poles supported the cloth that was extended to create a roof for the arena.

VELARIUM
This awning protected spectators from the sun and rain.

STATUES
The exterior facade was decorated with statues.

Animals into the Arena

Animals could appear unexpectedly in the arena from the *hypogeum*, by means of a mechanism activated with pulleys.

Vast Stage

At 289 feet (88 meters) long, 512 feet (156 meters) wide, and 157 feet (48 meters) tall, the stage had multiple arches and vaults. It was built using bricks, concrete, marble, travertine, and calcareous tufa.

SEATS

The areas for citizens had marble seats.

PORTICO

Made from wood, the portico protected the higher levels of the stands.

 STANDS

The spectators were situated according to social hierarchy: nobles in the lower area; women, the poor, and slaves in the upper area.

 ARENA

This measured 249 feet (76 meters) by 144 feet (44 meters). The floor was of wood. The framework of passages and the cells of the *hypogeum* were situated below.

Gladiators

Gladiatorial fights were the main attraction of the Colosseum. The belief that the life of the vanquished was pardoned by a thumbs-up gesture is an erroneous one.

3 **GALLERIES**

Vomitoria gave access to passages below the stands, which allowed for the evacuation of the public within minutes.

Strange Beasts

Spectacles less bloody than lion fights included the reproduction of natural landscapes, with animals that were exotic to the Romans, such as large elephants.

Stars of Antiquity

The gladiators of ancient Rome came from the lowest social classes: they were slaves, criminals, or prisoners. On the other hand, they earned money as payment for their work and if they were successful, they could gain their liberty. The most famous among them enjoyed some of the pleasures reserved for the highest strata of society; they were also considered heroes by the masses, who treated the most successful combatants as true stars. They could even become favorites of women in high society. In exceptional cases, free men became gladiators, but that was frowned upon by society. Although they were not at all common, female gladiators did exist.

Diverse Gladiators

The word "gladiator" derives from *gladius*, the ancient Romans' short sword. The first gladiatorial show took place in the year 264 BC. To begin with, between one and three pairs fought at the same time. However, Julius Caesar organized the first massive fights, with up to three hundred pairs of combatants simultaneously. The emperor Titus (at the end of the first century AD) organized exhausting spectacles, which lasted for up to one hundred days. Trajan, in the year 107, produced a colossal confrontation of 5,000 pairs of gladiators, to commemorate a military victory. There were at least fifteen types of gladiators, identified by their arms and equipment. These included: the *bestiario* (who fought against animals), *venator* (who hunted animals instead of fighting against them), *eques* (a horseback rider), *murmillo* (the most typical, wearing a helmet with a grilled visor), *retiarius* (armed with a trident and net), *secutor* (usually put up against the *retiarius*), and *laquearius* (who used a lasso).

SHORT, USEFUL LIFE
A gladiator's average lifetime did not exceed thirty years. If he survived as a fighter for between three and five years, he could gain his liberty.

ESTABLISHED PAIRS
It was established in advance which types of gladiators could confront each other.

Training and Fighting Equipment

Apprenticeships took place in a *ludus*, or "school." A few years passed before the trainee was ready to fight. The city of Rome had four schools. The biggest accommodated 2,000 fighters, dressed up with their combat equipment.

MASK
This mask belonged to a *gallus* gladiator (from Gaul). It was made of bronze and was used at the end of the first century BC.

HELMET
A characteristic helmet of the *murmillo*, the crest and the edge of the helmet resembled a fish.

GREAVES
Armor protected the knees and calves. They belonged to a Thracian gladiator from the first century BC.

Life or Death

The spectacles were not organized by the state, but privately, by an *editor*, who could be the emperor himself. The *editor* decided whether to pardon the life of a defeated man, taking into account the wishes of the spectators.

THE PUBLIC
Those attending the spectacle wore their best clothes, and could only enter with a *tessera* (invitation).

TRIUMPHAL EXIT
Victorious gladiators left the arena through the Porta Triumphalis.

VENATIONES
Here the gladiators hunted or fought duels with exotic wild animals. At the inauguration of the Colosseum, 9,000 beasts died.

ANCIENT GLADIATOR
The name *Samnite*, a people conquered by Rome, was derived from Samnium. This was one of the first types of gladiator.

CODE OF HONOR
The conquered gladiator, kneeling, recognized his defeat. If it was decided he should die, the code of conduct prevented him from crying out or showing any fear.

Spectacle of its Age

As its name indicates, the Circus Maximus, which was constructed in the sixth century BC, was the biggest stadium in Rome, and also the first circus in the city. It was a racetrack, designed for chariot racing, a sport and spectacle that the Romans took from the Greeks (it was one of the main attractions of the ancient Olympic Games). The stadium measured 2,037 feet (621 meters) in length and 387 feet (118 meters) in width. It was originally built in wood, but after successive alterations, in the year AD 103 the emperor Trajan authorized a final colossal structure in concrete and marble. It is believed that the capacity of the stadium was 150,000 seated spectators, but Pliny the Elder speaks of 250,000 people attending.

Slaves and Heroes

Normally, the races lasted for seven rounds, with twelve chariots, each having four horses. The different four-horse chariots (*quadrigae*) belonged to four established teams, identified by colors: green, red, blue, and white. The reins were tied to the belt of the *aurigae* (charioteers), who carried a curved knife to cut the reins in case of accident. Like the gladiators, the *aurigae* were slaves. If they were successful, they could obtain their liberty, as well as becoming great celebrities. The most famous *auriga* was Gaius Appuleius

Diocles, who retired at the age of forty-two after winning 1,462 races. He is considered the best-paid athlete in history: his winnings would be equivalent today to the unimaginable sum of fifteen billion dollars!

TOWERS
These towers marked the corners of the starting posts.

STARTING SIGNAL
The magistrate in charge of the spectacle threw a cloth (*mappa*) from here to start races.

STARTING BARRIER
The mechanism of the barrier used allowed the twelve gates to be opened at the same time.

SPINA (MEDIAN STRIP)
This low wall divided the track between the chariot turning points.

ENTRANCE
A procession that started the games entered here. The triple arch commemorated the taking of Jerusalem by Titus.

The Stadium

As well as chariot races, gladiatorial contests were held, including fighting against wild animals and other spectacles, which became less frequent when the Colosseum was built. The 1,130-foot (344-meter)-long central base (the *spina*) was adorned with statues, and sculpted eggs marked how many circuits had been covered in the competition. Later, another system for calculating circuits was added in the form of dolphins.

1 START
The end closest to the starting line was bigger to give the chariots space to line up.

2 PUBLIC
The seats were not booked in advance, and people also watched the show from the hills.

3 IMPERIAL BOX
This area connected with the Palatine Imperial Palace. The Colosseum stood behind it.

4 OBELISK
The obelisk was brought by the emperor Augustus from Heliopolis, Egypt. It was Rome's first obelisk.

TRACK
The track was covered in rolled sand.

EXTERIOR
The circus was three floors high, with arches and columns covered with marble.

Deadly Competition

The fragility of the chariots, and the light clothes worn by the drivers, made the races an extremely risky practice.

Reconstruction

Toward the year 50 BC, Julius Caesar extended the measurements of the circus to its maximum size. Later fires led to Trajan rebuilding it in stone.

JULIUS CAESAR
One of the promoters of public spectacles.

The Art of Governing

L eadership has been evident in all stages of humanity, and ancient civilizations gave preference to different specific requirements for their rulers. The Assyrians and Persians emphasized the military and strategic gifts of their leaders, while the Athenians also valued their magistrates' ability as orators. In Rome, the heads of patrician families were the only people with political rights, and they served the Senate for life, a state of affairs that gave great stability to this institution. Its functions were wide-reaching—embracing military affairs, external politics, economic questions, and public worship.

An Honorific Post

In antiquity, numerous thinkers offered theoretical models of the ideal ruler. In general, these models served as a basis for the education of the privileged sectors, who were the only individuals with the possibility of holding government posts. Among the Egyptians, the top magistrates would retain their posts only if they showed a capacity to unquestionably obey the pharaoh's orders and to carry out their duties efficiently. The Greeks were convinced that governing was one of the most noble of human activities, and they believed that politicians had to be the best—that is, to have the highest morals—to dedicate their lives to the common good. In the sixth century BC, the Roman patricians, who considered themselves heirs to the founders of the city, consolidated themselves as the only decision makers capable of managing the state. They established a republican system of government, whose principal aims were to maintain the division of power and to avoid the abuse of authority.

LICTORS
Officers who assisted the magistrates.

Cursus Honorum

Political ascent of Roman citizens was regulated by the *cursus honorum* (course of offices). This was the sequence of public offices that politicians held, from consul to *censor*. The posts were usually held for a period of one year.

A **CONSUL**
Two consuls were elected at a time. They commanded the army and held executive power.

B **PRAETOR**
The *praetor* administered justice and assisted the two consuls with legal advice.

C **AEDILE**
The *aedile* handled municipal administration and provisions for the whole city.

D **QUAESTOR**
The *quaestor* dealt with finance, economic administration, and tax.

E **CENSOR**
The *censor* classified citizens by their riches and stipulated the taxes due.

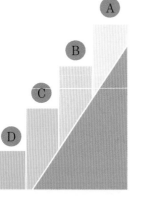

The Roman Senate

The Senate represented the true political center of Rome. Three hundred patricians held posts for life; they directed foreign affairs, decided the rate of taxes, and controlled the consuls.

Homicides

Julius Caesar was stabbed to death by a group of legislators in the grounds of the Senate, in March of the year 44 BC.

1 CONSULS
Military and political command was the job of the consuls (magistrates). Their appointment could be extended by the Roman Senate.

2 SENATORS
The senators were instructed in various rhetorical techniques to improve their speeches and skills of persuasion within the auditorium.

Leaders of other Civilizations

Cyrus the Great founded the Achaemenid Empire, the largest in all of antiquity, making use of his strategic gifts and charismatic leadership. Moreover, he defended religious tolerance toward conquered peoples, basing this on Zoroastrianism. Pericles was a Greek politician, from the fifth century BC, who ran the government of Athens with enthusiasm, becoming a promoter of the recently consolidated popular democracy.

PERSONAL RING
They used one of iron on the ring finger of the right hand.

WEARING A TOGA
This was a privilege exclusive to members of the Senate.

DISTINCTION
Senators wore *calcei*, red or black sandals, with buckles.

The Best in History

The legend that describes the brothers Romulus and Remus as its founders puts the birth of Rome at 754 BC. Some historians affirm it was some time in the eighth century BC, although archaeological finds suggest the city had arisen in the tenth century. Beyond that date of origin, it is certain that a group of Latins founded a settlement on Mount Palatine, close to the Tiber River, a strategic place for commerce in the region, which in time would extend to the other six surrounding hills. At first, it was a small village, then a city, and finally the most important empire in history. The Roman army played a fundamental role in this transformation.

The Early Times

After breaking free from Etruscan domination, Rome established its own army. As was usual in that era (around 509 BC), the Greek model was adopted: citizens got their combat equipment; they were mobilized if there was a war; and they fought in a phalanx. The function of the Roman army was to defend the city from attacks by its neighbors. In the fourth century BC, the Republic moved onto the offensive, subduing the other Latin peoples of the region, including the Etruscans, the Sabines, the Osci, and the Samnites, among others. In that very war against those last mentioned (300 BC),

there was an important tactical change; the formation of a phalanx was replaced by the formation of *maniples*. Instead of lining up in a long, wide mass of combatants, they came together in blocks of 120–200 soldiers. This tactic was successful with the Greeks, but failed against the Carthaginians in the Second Punic War. For this reason, they improved it even further; the maniples were distributed in three lines, positioned in the battlefield as if they were on a chess board (*acies*). This formation—triple battle order (*triplex acies*)—provided them with the capacity to maneuver and tactical flexibility without losing strength.

The Allies

As well as the *maniple*, there also appeared the *ala*, or wing—a formation similar to the Roman one but made up from the *socii*, Rome's Italian allies. A Roman consular army from this age consisted of two legions and two wings. In the third century BC, heavy cavalry squadrons (*equites*) were added, which covered each side of the formation, and also some mercenary troops, such as Cretan archers, who responded to specific needs.

BRAVERY IN VAIN
Courage did not compensate for poor discipline.

DIFFERENT WEAPONS
Rome's enemies were well armed, but they did not use their weapons tactically.

Village to Empire

Rome arose as a small hamlet on the edge of the Tiber River to become an empire that extended from Great Britain to the Sahara, and from Portugal to Iraq. This empire existed for more than 600 years, thanks to the incredible capacity of the Roman legions—without doubt the most efficient warriors in the whole of history.

Difficult to Wear Down

For the Romans, the British Isles were a difficult nut to crack. Their first attempts at invasion were made by Caesar in 55 and 54 BC. Later, in AD 43, the slow process of true conquest started. However, the situation remained generally unstable. The northern frontier was demarcated by Hadrian's Wall (above), which protected conquered Britain from the warlike Picts.

KINGDOM (EIGHTH AND SEVENTH CENTURIES BC)
Rome scarcely occupied the area of the city and its surroundings.

REPUBLIC (SIXTH TO FIRST CENTURY BC)
Rome dominated the Italian Peninsula, the Iberian Peninsula, Gaul, Greece, Palestine, and North Africa.

EMPIRE (FIRST TO SIXTH CENTURY AD)
This reached an area estimated at no less than 2.5 million square miles (6.5 million square kilometers; see map above).

Order and Discipline

One of the greatest examples of the legions' capability was the battle of Watling Street, waged in AD 60 in what is modern-day Britain. Commanded by Suetonius, 10,000 Romans defeated Queen Boudicca's 70,000 Britons.

2 MEDIEVAL HISTORY

Medieval History

In early medieval times, the different continents developed at very different paces and quite separately from each other. Europe sat in the Dark Ages following the collapse of the Western Roman Empire, while Muslim and Asian cultures enjoyed a period of stunning scientific progress. When the West eventually caught up with technological and agricultural innovations that allowed commerce to flourish and the population to grow, the stage was set for the Age of Discovery and Europe's cultural renaissance.

MEDIEVAL ASIA

The vast Asiatic territory of the Middle Ages witnessed the rise of some empires and the decline of others. It was an era of formidable armies, with unique characteristics very different to those of their counterparts in the West.

Early Middle Ages
FAMILY UNITS

Most peasant families in medieval Europe were basically economic units. The choice of a spouse was not determined by love or affection, but instead by the interests involved in developing the family economy.

Early Middle Ages
LIFE EXPECTANCY

Average life expectancy in medieval Europe was thirty years, and those older than forty-five were considered elderly. Most female deaths occurred between the ages of fifteen and thirty and were due to puerperal fever or difficult childbirth. The birth rate was high; infant survival rate very low.

Eighth Century
CAMELS

Early evidence suggests that the domestication of camels happened in North Africa around the third century. It was not until the eighth century, however, that it was introduced on a mass scale, revolutionizing trans-Saharan trade.

1254–1324
MARCO POLO

The famous Venetian traveler spent seventeen years in service to the Mongol emperor and was imprisoned by the Genoans on his return. Publication of the book *The Travels of Marco Polo* was the unveiling of the Far East for Europe.

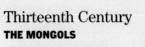

Thirteenth Century
THE MONGOLS

Under the leadership of Genghis Khan, the Mongols created the second major empire in history, governing more than 100 million people over a vast area of 13.5 million square miles (35 million square kilometers). They achieved this thanks to their army, which made a religion out of mobility and logistics.

Fifteenth Century
KOREAN SUN CLOCKS

Jang Yeong-sil, who lived during the Joseon dynasty, was one of the most important inventors in the Far East. His sun clocks (left) were scattered throughout Seoul, allowing the city's inhabitants to check the time.

Sixth Century Onward
MONASTERIES

The first monasteries adhered to the Benedictine Rule, established by St. Benedict in 529. Monastic orders differed mainly in the details of their religious observation and how strictly they applied their rules, but they all formed independent, self-supporting communities. As a monastery increased in wealth and numbers, it could grow to cover many acres and give the appearance of a fortified town.

Seventh Century Onward
MUSLIM CULTURE

Throughout the Middle Ages, Islam spread over the southern and eastern Mediterranean, a good part of Eastern Europe, Asia, and all of Africa. Muslim culture, with its scientific and literary knowledge, was dazzling. All Muslim children—male and female—attended elementary school to learn the Koran (left).

800–1300
CASTLES

Whether on the motte, in the bailey, inside the walls of the keep, or as a separate building within the great curtain walls of the thirteenth century, the living quarters of a castle invariably had one basic element: the great hall, where feudal lords would host large banquets. These feasts often had a political motivation, such as forging or cementing alliances in time of war.

1088
CHINESE INVENTIONS

While the West was stuck in the Middle Ages, the East, in particular China, was forging ahead with a stream of scientific and technological inventions. Su Song, a government employee and engineer, constructed his water-driven astronomical clock tower (left) in 1088.

Europe 1000–1200
A NEW URBAN LANDSCAPE

The flow of foreign invasions had stopped, the productivity of the land had increased, towns had been established, and commerce expanded. A new social class—the middle class—grew, as did cities; guild schools, cathedral schools, parish schools, and universities all became part of the emerging urban landscape.

Fourteenth Century
THE AZTECS

The Aztecs of Central America were a warrior people who established a complex society and worshipped ancestors and gods. They developed forms of writing, erected astonishing architectural structures, and achieved mathematical and astrological supremacy.

1337–1453
HUNDRED YEARS WAR

The Hundred Years War marked the beginning of the end of traditional knighthood. The victory of scarcely 6,000 Englishmen over a French force of 36,000 at Agincourt in 1415 prompted the rethinking of traditional weaponry and fighting methods, which hadn't changed much for centuries.

1397–1494
THE MEDICI BANK

It was in this bank of the powerful Florentine family that the so-called "double-entry bookkeeping" was developed, which proved to be a lasting and important contribution to the history of accounting.

Fifteenth Century
TRANSATLANTIC EXCHANGE

The arrival of Europeans in the Americas started a major revolution in global eating habits. The flow of products between the Old and New worlds, in both directions, transformed the flora and fauna and notably enriched the diet of the settlers in both regions.

Medieval Europe

The medieval period, spanning more than a millennium from 400–1500 AD, is the longest major era in European history. It is also exceedingly complex. Following the collapse of the Roman Empire, life in the early part of this period was notably more primitive—hence the "Dark Ages" epithet

sometimes attached to it. The period is further divided into three sub-eras: the Early Middle Ages (400–ca. 1000), the High Middle Ages (ca. 1000–1300), and the Late Middle Ages (1300–ca. 1450). In Britain, the beginning of the High Middle Ages can be dated to the Norman Invasion of 1066.

All for One

Families in medieval Europe consisted of the matrimonial nucleus of husband, wife, and children, as well as an extended group of relatives—for example widows, young orphans, nieces and nephews, and uncles and aunts. They all lived in the same dwelling, and devoted themselves to agricultural activities under the control of the feudal lord—the owner of the lands they worked and a member of the warrior nobility. The lords used to grant or reject permission for the peasants under their command to marry.

Union and Interests

Most medieval peasant families were, at the same time, units of production—that is, they were used to all working together for their livelihood. In general, it was not love and affection that determined who was selected as a partner for marriage but instead the families' economic interests. In this sense, the peasants' choice of marriage partner would frequently be influenced by the feudal lords—the landowners—on whose land they resided. The poorest people, who had no chance of owning their own property, went to work in the castles.

Feudal Lords

Lords enjoyed the right of *pernocte*, or "spending the night," which was the right to have sexual relations with any woman from the fiefdom on the night of her wedding.

LARGE FAMILY
Peasant families were bigger than families of the privileged classes. On average, they had six members, with different degrees of kinship.

WORK IN THE COUNTRYSIDE
Boys were more in demand than girls for working in the fields.

1

BREAST-FEEDING
This continued, as a food supplement, until the child was three or four years old.

1 FEUDAL SYMBOL

The fiefdom was the land that belonged to the feudal lords by inheritance or accord. The castles—fortresses dedicated to defense—were the residences of the lords, their families, warriors, and servants. At times of invasion, the peasants ran for shelter behind their walls.

2 FAMILY HOUSE

In the Middle Ages, poorer people lived together in one space with animals, implements, and food. All family members rested together on the ground, covered with straw, and stayed close together to keep warm during the night.

3 LIVING AND SURVIVING

Life expectancy was thirty years, and those older than forty-five were considered to have lived a long life. Most female deaths were due to puerperal fever, or difficult childbirth, which usually occurred between the ages of fifteen and thirty. The birth rate was high, but the survival rate very low.

4 NUMEROUS OFFSPRING

Medieval peasant families usually had many children. When they grew up, they would help with the collective rural and household tasks.

5 WITHIN THEIR MEANS

Homes were simple and built by the family group. They were limited in size and materials from the area were used.

PROTECTION OF MEMBERS
Peasant families were under the command of the feudal lord, who, it was assumed, had descended from noble lineage. Moreover, he would be obliged to protect them militarily.

ARMED CONFLICTS
An environment of constant fighting hampered production and family relations.

Time of Banquets

Castles were important venues in medieval Europe. They were built of stone, and courtly medieval families and their closest servants lived in them. The feudal lords were the chief authorities in the regions and they would organize numerous banquets to entertain their principal allies and loyal warriors. The dining room arrangements represented the hierarchical organization of society: the host and hostess and selected priests sat at the main table, and the less important vassals sat farther away. A religious blessing would precede the meal. When the noble gave the order, the servants would start to distribute wine and food to everyone present.

Food that Unites

The feudal lords wined and dined their guests with large banquets in their castles. Medieval times were characterized by constant wars and armed conflicts and, for that reason, the survival of courtly families depended on the quality of the relations they established with the warrior nobility. The main aim of banquets was to strengthen military bonds of loyalty and demonstrate power and riches. They provided a great variety of food, intermingled with music, dance, and theatrical performances. Meat was the most popular dish, given that, for reasons of religious tradition, its consumption was restricted for a large part of the year. Dishes were flavored by spices, which were considered to be luxury products reserved for special occasions; black pepper, cinnamon, and cumin were among the most commonly used. The most usual practice was to share glasses and bread, or to remove the platters, so a portion of food could be offered to fellow diners. The extreme religiosity of the age gave rise to a prohibition on throwing away food and, if there was too much, they had to give it to the poor.

DECORATION
Arms, shields, and tapestries were used for covering the stone walls.

Food and Protection

The peasants paid taxes by handing over food to their feudal lords in exchange for military protection. According to their means, they reared pheasants, hens, ducks, pigs, and goats in their domestic yards; these were then brought to the castle storeroom. They also produced cheese, milk, and dairy products.

HUNTING
Wild boars and pheasants were the most popular game.

SOUP
This was cooked in large pots with added leftovers.

HIERARCHIES
The top table was usually raised on a wooden platform.

Feasting in the Castle

Banquets were common in peacetime for the amusement of those family members who lived in the castle, and at times of war, as a way of developing strategies with military allies. The meals usually consisted of a first course of soup, and a second course of roasted meat or fish, accompanied by vegetables. Bread, dairy products, and eggs—essential foods to the diet—were produced in the surrounding countryside. Wine was usually the only drink.

1 FURNITURE
The tables were wooden slabs mounted on trestles. The main table had a tablecloth and polished dishes.

3 EATING WITH HANDS
Spoons and knives existed, but people were accustomed to tearing their food into pieces with both hands.

2 ENTERTAINMENTS
Banquets could go on for hours or days. Musicians and performers livened up the evenings with their shows.

4 FOR THE TOAST
The main drink was not water but wine. It was scented by adding some honey, thyme, or pepper.

DARK ROOMS
Castles did not have many windows: defense was the main priority.

Preserving Knowledge

The cities that were heirs to classical culture entered into decline in the Early Middle Ages, and with them went their educational practices. The process of the ruralization of society advanced, restrictions on slaves were relaxed, and feudalism was established as a means of production. Catholicism developed a far-reaching campaign of evangelization, buildings and libraries from antiquity were destroyed, and the Roman Church was established as the new, main handler of education.

Monasteries

At the start of the sixth century in Italy, the priest Benedict of Nursia founded the Order of St. Benedict, whose function was to establish monasteries throughout Christendom. They had to be self-sufficient, so productive activity was essential. They also had to be built as isolated and protected structures, where the monks could withdraw in prayer for the salvation of souls. Their maxim was "Ora et labora" (Pray and work). The abbot was the head of the monastery, and he watched to ensure that the rule was being observed, assigning tasks to the rest of the monks. The *regula monasteriorum*, better known as the Rule of St. Benedict, was established, which determined how the monastery functioned overall. The monks had to pray at set times, carry out agricultural work, and participate in the choir, as well as complete other tasks, such as preserving and copying ancient books.

Monte Cassino

The first scriptorium was established by the priest Benedict of Nursia himself, in his monastery at Monte Cassino—situated to the south of Rome—in the year 529.

OUTLYING GRANARY
To avoid pests.

WALLS
Fortification, for defense and isolation.

CELLS
Individual and with few objects, for the monks to dedicate themselves to prayer.

LIBRARY
Facing the sunrise, to make the most of the light.

DINING HALL
While eating, the monks listened to religious readings.

Scriptorium

A room in large monasteries, used for copying and transcribing books, its aim was to expand on examples preserved from antiquity.

LIGHTING

Large windows and oil lamps illuminated the room.

PRINCIPAL MONK

He coordinated tasks, often according to a rota, and directed prayers.

HEATING

The scriptorium was close to the kitchens to keep the workplace well heated.

SITUATION

The scriptorium was close to the library, where books that were to be copied were preserved on parchment.

LECTERN

The monks were stationed at individual lecterns, in silence, with their copying tools.

Miniatures

The monks not only copied books, but illustrated them, too. Letters and titles were decorated with filigree and included fantastical animals, such as dragons and unicorns. They also inserted illustrations of landscapes of the day.

MODIFICATIONS

The monks often added commentaries to the books they copied.

BOOKS

The parchment scrolls and books were preserved in cupboards.

Emerging Universities

Between the eleventh and thirteenth centuries, Europe was passing through a new cycle of expansion and prosperity. Feudalism as a political and economic form of rule had been consolidated, the stream of foreign invasions had stopped, the productivity of the land had increased because of the use of new technology, towns had been established, and commerce expanded. Thus a new social class arose—the middle class—dedicated to that activity. In addition, the cities grew again and reconstituted themselves as the main educational centers of the period. Guild schools, cathedral schools, and parish schools, together with elementary school teachers and universities, were, inevitably, all part of the new urban landscape.

Learning in the Borough

While the old educational ways were maintained in rural places, in the cities new educational practices were being established. The parish schools, which leaned toward the Church, taught the catechism and a smattering of reading, writing, and calculus. The cathedral schools, which were founded by bishops, were for the training of lay monks; classes took place in the cathedral cloisters. These schools taught more elaborate forms of knowledge, including geometry, rhetoric, and grammar. Universities were created toward the twelfth century. Some arose from a body of teachers (Paris), and others from a body of students who were looking for teachers (Bologna). The first example was the Faculty of Arts, where the *trivium* and *quadrivium* were taught—curricula used in antiquity. The first included "humanistic" knowledge: grammar, dialectics, and rhetoric; and the second included "realistic" knowledge: arithmetic, geometry, astronomy, and music. Upon finishing, students could continue with studies in canonical or civil law, medicine, or theology; it depended on the universities, given that these three courses were not taught in all of them. The length of study for a theologian could be up to fifteen years or more.

Guild Schools

Urban workers organized themselves in guilds. There, they trained new members, who started as apprentices. They then became officials, until, having produced their "masterpiece," they acquired the right to practice the profession.

The Teaching of Medicine

Some universities, such as Salerno in Italy or Montpellier in France, specialized in medical training. The use of human cadavers for teaching anatomy came later. Before that, animals, such as pigs, were used.

HIPPOCRATES AND GALEN
Classical doctors were the point of reference.

AUTOPSIES
Animals and humans were dissected to learn about anatomy.

LEVELS
Each student could graduate as a bachelor, a master, or a doctor.

The Magisterial Class

These classes were based on the *lectio* (where the educator explained or read a text), the *quaestiones* (where he presented the arguments), and the *disputatio* (where the topics were commented on). The pupils took notes in their notebooks and answered the teacher's questions.

BOARDING
The students lived together in halls of residence nearby.

1 PUPILS
Access to the magisterial class was free for white Catholic men. There was no obligatory age of entry; it varied from fourteen to twenty years of age.

2 EDUCATOR
Many lecturers at the front of the magisterial classes were priests, who might belong to a regular or a secular order.

3 CHAIR
The teacher sat on a privileged seat of honor in front of the class, from where he gave his lessons. The location symbolized his unquestionable knowledge.

4 GUARDIAN
The guardian was responsible for keeping order and discipline, and for assisting the lecturer during the class.

UNIVERSITY PRESTIGE
The University of Oxford came about because of a royal decree preventing English people from attending the University of Paris. The University of Cambridge was the result of a schism; a group of academics moved away from Oxford because of disagreements with the authorities.

STUDY CARDS
The courses taught by the teachers have survived in written form.

BOOKBINDING
The exercise books were made of sheepskin, folded into four sheets.

GRADUATION
On successful completion, a ceremony took place in which the graduate was given a series of objects, such as a gown and a tasseled cap.

A Window on the Far East

A symbol of the trade routes between the West and the Far East, the Silk Road was the name given by history and geography students, during the nineteenth century, to a group of routes that united remote China with Europe, across Central Asia. Silk was certainly transported along the route. However, there were all kinds of other items, too, including less tangible ones, such as ideas, philosophical trends, religions, and inventions, as yet unknown to one side of the world or the other.

The Impossible Voyage

Silk was a luxury item; it was sumptuous, and its manufacture was, for centuries, a secret jealously guarded by the Chinese. Recent archaeological records show that the art of silk production goes back at least 5,000 years, and that thousands of years ago methods of exchange already existed between Europe and China, which included items made of silk. However, a real route was not developed until the second century BC—first, at the hands of diplomats sent on official missions, but then, quickly, at the hands of merchants, generally from kingdoms in Central Asia. Perfumes, jewels, and decorative pieces of glass were transported on the backs of camels, traveling in large caravans and crossing the snow-covered mountain ranges, to trade with silk goods in China, which were taken back with them to the West. Crossing the famous route, and returning, was a one- or two-year journey filled with danger and unforeseen events; however, it was worth it. In the commercial centers of the West, for example, Byzantium and Rome itself, silk was worth a fortune, and this made merchants rich. The route declined rapidly, and later, toward the fifteenth century, fell into disuse.

EARLY YEARS
Along the entire Silk Road, trade tended to be in the hands of merchants from the kingdoms of Sogdiana (currently Tajikistan and Uzbekistan), Kushan (Afghanistan, India, Pakistan, and Tajikistan), and the Parthian regions.

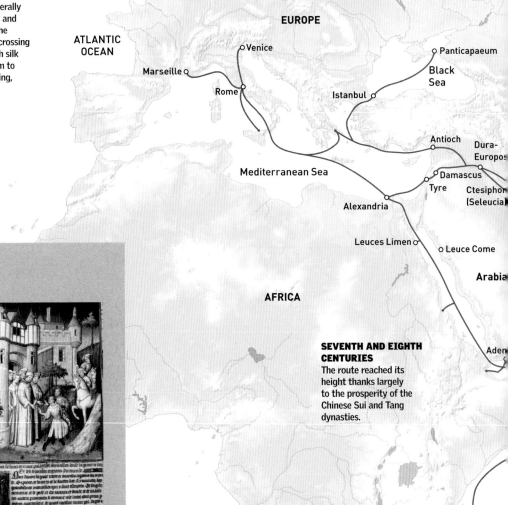

ATLANTIC
OCEAN

EUROPE

Venice

Marseille

Rome

Panticapaeum

Black
Sea

Istanbul

Antioch

Dura-
Europos

Damascus

Mediterranean Sea

Tyre

Ctesiphon
(Seleucia)

Alexandria

Leuces Limen

Leuce Come

Arabia

AFRICA

SEVENTH AND EIGHTH CENTURIES
The route reached its height thanks largely to the prosperity of the Chinese Sui and Tang dynasties.

Aden

An All-Time Classic

The Million, later called *The Travels of Marco Polo*, was written (perhaps in 1298) by Rustichello of Pisa, a prison-cell companion of the great traveler, based on his stories along the Silk Road. The book, which was really a kind of manual for merchants, opened the eyes of the West to the marvels of the East, and became a classic, even before the invention of printing.

Technical Secrets

Various legends, which include princesses, smugglers, and Byzantine monk thieves, tell how the technique of making silk was revealed to other people in Central Asia, who produced the thread regularly toward the fifth century.

1 The worm is grown under the best conditions, until it covers itself in silk to start its metamorphosis.

2 The cocoon is woven from one single, very long thread—finer than a hair—covered with a sticky substance.

3 Before the moths leave the cocoons, they are placed in boiling water. This kills the larvae and dilutes the sticky substance.

4 Once the process is complete, the silk thread is easily disentangled from the cocoon.

5 The thread is soaked in oil and spun into a form that makes it strong.

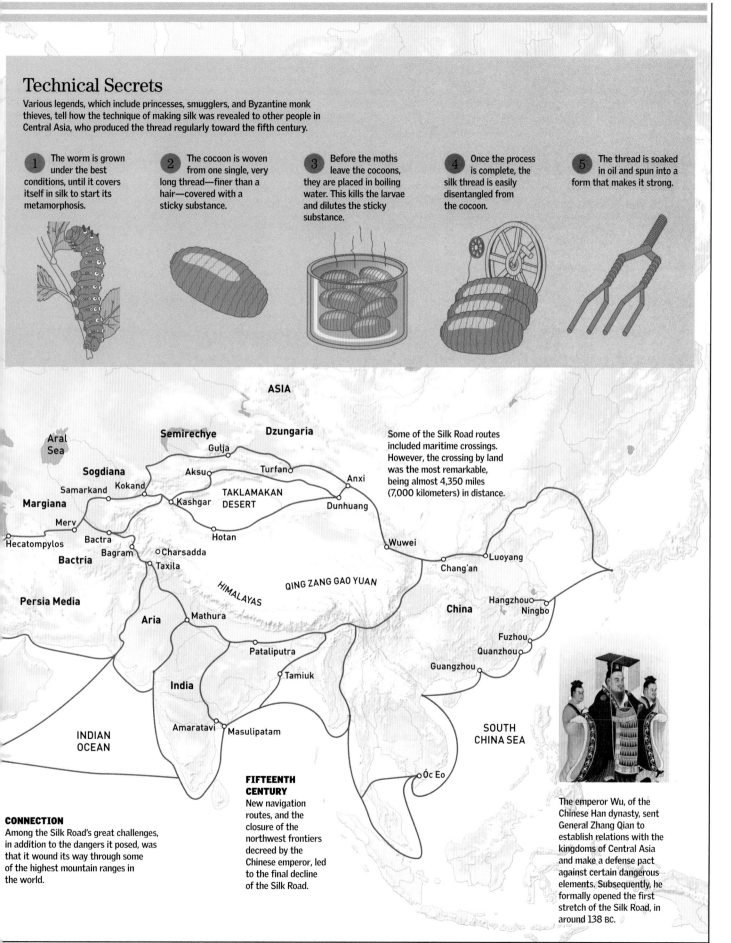

ASIA

Aral Sea

Semirechye

Dzungaria

Gulja

Sogdiana

Aksu

Turfan

Anxi

Margiana

Samarkand

Kokand

Kashgar

TAKLAMAKAN DESERT

Dunhuang

Merv

Hotan

Wuwei

Hecatompylos

Bactra

Bagram

Charsadda

Taxila

HIMALAYAS

QING ZANG GAO YUAN

Chang'an

Luoyang

Bactria

Persia Media

Aria

Mathura

China

Hangzhou

Ningbo

Fuzhou

Pataliputra

Quanzhou

Tamiuk

Guangzhou

India

INDIAN OCEAN

Amaratavi

Masulipatam

SOUTH CHINA SEA

Óc Eo

Some of the Silk Road routes included maritime crossings. However, the crossing by land was the most remarkable, being almost 4,350 miles (7,000 kilometers) in distance.

FIFTEENTH CENTURY
New navigation routes, and the closure of the northwest frontiers decreed by the Chinese emperor, led to the final decline of the Silk Road.

CONNECTION
Among the Silk Road's great challenges, in addition to the dangers it posed, was that it wound its way through some of the highest mountain ranges in the world.

The emperor Wu, of the Chinese Han dynasty, sent General Zhang Qian to establish relations with the kingdoms of Central Asia and make a defense pact against certain dangerous elements. Subsequently, he formally opened the first stretch of the Silk Road, in around 138 BC.

Heart of the Middle Ages

Venice, famous now for being an enchanting tourist enclave, with its canals, little bridges, and gondolas, was once perhaps the greatest commercial power in the world. The Venetians were, above all, merchants, and they traded intially through the Mediterranean, then later through the rest of Europe, until they reached the Middle East, Central Asia, and the Far East by means of the Silk Road. The sixteenth century was the beginning of the end for independent Venice, which became, after three centuries, part of the Kingdom of Italy.

Exchange— An Obsession

Founded toward the beginning of the fifth century and established on a small lagoon situated between the Italian coast and the Adriatic Sea, Venice grew rapidly as a marginal stronghold for people expelled from continental Europe. In scarcely four centuries, the magnificent diplomatic and commercial capacity of its inhabitants had transformed it into a republic, truly independent from both the Holy Roman Empire and the Byzantine Empire. The Venetians were not interested in annexing territory to build a great empire, but instead in the freedom to trade. Thus, with the products they exchanged, they came to be present not only throughout Europe, but also throughout the limits of the known world, including the Far East, due to their domination of the so-called Silk Road. The marvelous stories of Marco Polo, a thirteenth-century Venetian trader, and the way he discovered China, India, and Persia for the West, provide but a small indication of those times of glory.

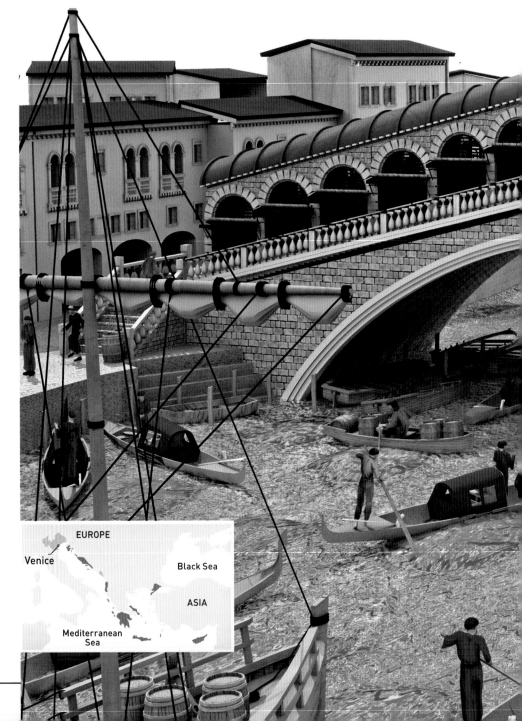

Almost an Empire
During the fifteenth century, Venice experienced its greatest territorial expansion, with important possessions along the Mediterranean and enormous influence in commercial ports, in places as far distant as the Black Sea or the North Sea coasts.

EUROPE

Venice

Black Sea

ASIA

Mediterranean Sea

Gold Ducat

Toward the end of the thirteenth century, Venice's power had increased to such an extent that a new coin was introduced: the gold ducat. This coin was destined to become the most important in Europe, at least over the course of two or three centuries.

Medieval Venice

Venetian power was evident in scenes of everyday life, where it was normal to see its inhabitants dressed luxuriously.

Slave Trade

Among the enormous variety of products traded by the Venetians, one of the most profitable was slaves, in spite of prohibition by the Church. Slaves were obtained in southern Russia to sell in North Africa, and also from North Africa to sell in Europe.

REASONS FOR TRADE
Due to its limited size, the territory of Venice lacked its own manufacturing. Therefore, the Venetians excelled at exchanging products created by others.

Venice of the North

The commercial city par excellence in medieval times was Venice. However, the extremely important role played by Bruges between the twelfth century and the sixteenth century is often underestimated. Even so, for many researchers, it had become the "Venice of the North." Bruges was criss-crossed by a large number of canals and bridges; it was also central for the traffic of goods between the Roman and Germanic worlds within Western Europe, as well as being the port of entrance and exit for Central and Eastern Europe.

The Heart of Medieval Europe

Even in the twelfth century, Bruges had turned into the main port of northeast Europe, and head of the London Hansa, or Hanseatic League—a confederation of Flemish cities that handled the imports of wool from England. By the thirteenth century, however, another powerful confederation—the Teutonic Hansa, which handled all the commerce toward the

Baltic Sea, passing through the Nordic countries—established one of its most important commercial centers in Bruges. The city experienced an explosion. The English wool trade was centered on Bruges. Some of the wool was made into clothing, which was distributed throughout the rest of Europe and the Mediterranean, in a similar way to the products that arrived from the Teutonic

League. At the same time, products from the Mediterranean arrived at Bruges to be distributed to the British Isles and toward the Baltic, in a plan that would be preserved until the beginning of the sixteenth century, when Bruges entered into noticeable decline.

CRANES
Cranes with belts, driven by human traction, were used to load certain goods onto the boats—for example, wine from the French region of Gascony.

CARTS
Carts were used for transporting the goods on land.

DOCKERS
Men working as dockers loaded and unloaded boats in the port.

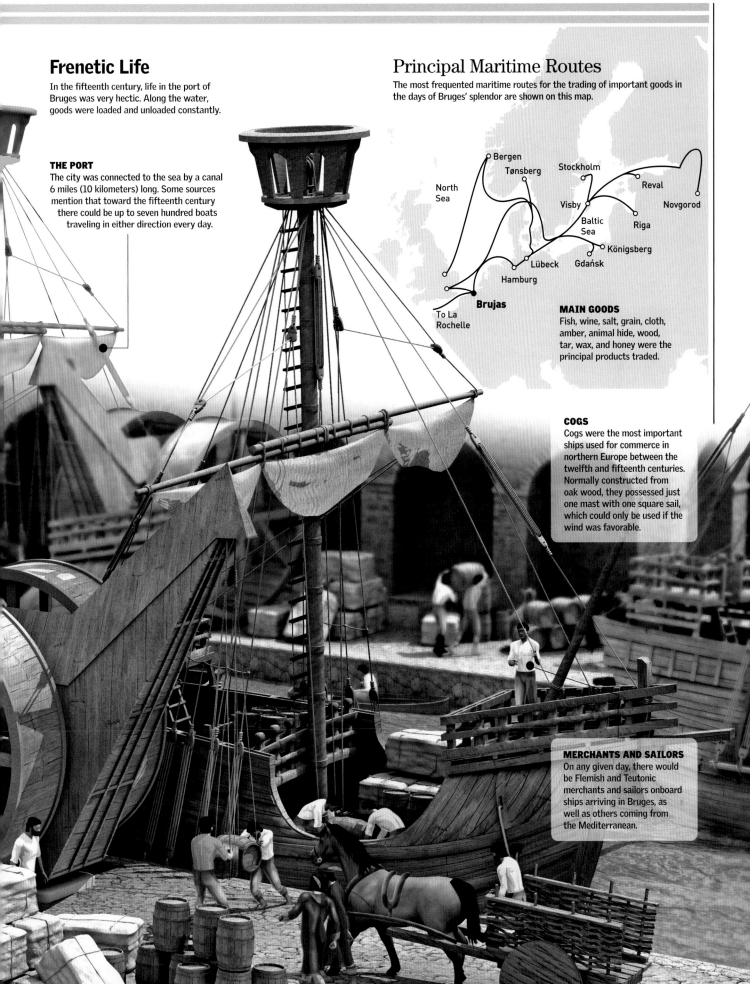

Frenetic Life

In the fifteenth century, life in the port of Bruges was very hectic. Along the water, goods were loaded and unloaded constantly.

THE PORT
The city was connected to the sea by a canal 6 miles (10 kilometers) long. Some sources mention that toward the fifteenth century there could be up to seven hundred boats traveling in either direction every day.

Principal Maritime Routes

The most frequented maritime routes for the trading of important goods in the days of Bruges' splendor are shown on this map.

Bergen
Tønsberg
Stockholm
North Sea
Reval
Novgorod
Visby
Baltic Sea
Riga
Königsberg
Lübeck
Gdańsk
Hamburg
Brujas
To La Rochelle

MAIN GOODS
Fish, wine, salt, grain, cloth, amber, animal hide, wood, tar, wax, and honey were the principal products traded.

COGS
Cogs were the most important ships used for commerce in northern Europe between the twelfth and fifteenth centuries. Normally constructed from oak wood, they possessed just one mast with one square sail, which could only be used if the wind was favorable.

MERCHANTS AND SAILORS
On any given day, there would be Flemish and Teutonic merchants and sailors onboard ships arriving in Bruges, as well as others coming from the Mediterranean.

Honor and Combat

During the Middle Ages in Western Europe, kings depended on small private armies belonging to the feudal lords to sustain their power. These were made up of medieval knights: warriors on horseback—mostly young and of noble origin—who served their lords for glory, honor, titles, land, and money, and who generally lacked patriotic vision. The Crusades saw a new motivation, a religious one, while the Hundred Years War marked the decline of the knight as a combatant.

Heavy Armory

Despite the fact that the medieval period lasted many centuries, the weaponry and the fighting methods used by medieval knights barely changed over the years. The horse, the suit of armor, the helmet, the shield, the spear, and the sword were their basic equipment. The characteristic combat strategy was to charge. Feudal armies formed in three corps: vanguard, center, and rearguard; and they rushed forward, charging, one by one, in waves. The idea was to make their way through the enemy ranks, taking advantage of the momentum, weight, and speed of the onrush. Starting at a trot, they then sped up until reaching a gallop. The knights attacked with spears, and, if those broke, they used their sword or mace. The appearance of the crossbow and the long bow, with arrows capable of easily penetrating a suit of armor, placed the medieval knight under threat. On October 25, 1415, against the backdrop of the Hundred Years War, the English forces of Henry V, with scarcely 6,000 men, of which some 5,000 were archers, decisively defeated the French army—a force of 36,000, of which 10,000 were knights. It was the beginning of the end of the age of knighthood.

The Crusades

Probably the greatest armies of knights in the Middle Ages were the multinational armies of crusaders, who tried to seize the Holy Land from the hands of Islam.

The Art of Arming Themselves

Getting dressed in a suit of armor, with its hundreds of pieces and enormous weight, was a tedious task, for which the knight needed assistance. It was even necessary sometimes to hoist the knight with a crane to get him onto his horse.

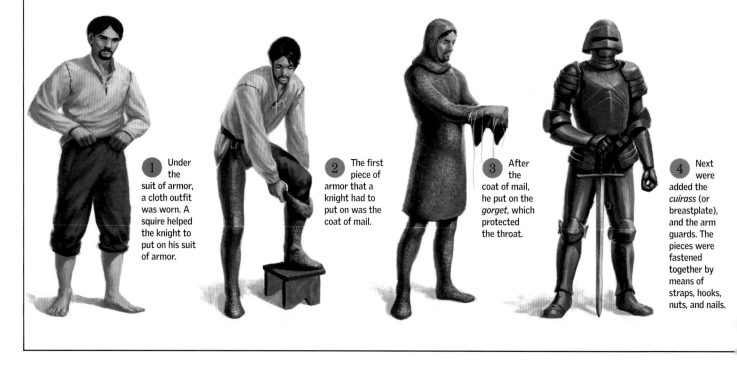

1 Under the suit of armor, a cloth outfit was worn. A squire helped the knight to put on his suit of armor.

2 The first piece of armor that a knight had to put on was the coat of mail.

3 After the coat of mail, he put on the gorget, which protected the throat.

4 Next were added the *cuirass* (or breastplate), and the arm guards. The pieces were fastened together by means of straps, hooks, nuts, and nails.

The Suit of Armor

Between the tenth and twelfth centuries, knights used only a coat of mail, a helmet, and a shield as armor. At the end of the twelfth century, they started to add metal plates to protect certain parts of the body. By the fourteenth century, they wore a complete suit of armor. The invention of gunpowder and firearms, however, made this obsolete.

HELMET
Some helmets were made out of just one piece of metal. Others had retractable visors to protect the face. They usually had internal protection.

GORGET AND BEVOR
The *gorget* covered the neck, the throat, and the thorax; the *bevor*, the jaw and the mouth.

TOO MUCH WEIGHT
A suit of armor ended up having 250 metallic pieces, and could weigh more than 100 pounds (50 kilograms). The armed knight weighed so much that it was difficult for him to move, and if he fell from his horse, he was defenseless.

TOTAL PROTECTION
Large shoulder plates covered the shoulders; arm guards, the upper arms; elbow plates, the elbow; and bracers, the arm and the forearm.

The Sword

A sword was used for man-to-man combat, because its point could go through almost any suit of armor of the time. It had a straight blade of tempered steel, with a double cutting edge.

COAT OF MAIL
The mail was formed by joining together small metallic disks.

GREAT SIZE
The sword was 30–33 inches (75–85 centimeters) long and it weighed 3–3½ pounds (1.3–1.5 kg).

CUISSES
These protected the thighs; the *greaves* were for the lower part of the legs; other pieces protected the calves.

Medieval Asia

edieval Asia far surpassed the West in the development of technology for use in warfare, science, and the arts. The Chinese were using gunpowder as early as the eleventh century, and they had movable-type printing five hundred years before Europe. During this era, the

continent was largely dominated by the Mongol Empire, with Genghis Khan and his grandson, Kublai Khan, controlling lands from Eastern Europe to the Sea of Japan. Angkor Wat in Cambodia, the Great South Gate in Japan, and the Tianning Temple in China are some of the surviving architectural masterpieces from this period.

Baghdad

Founded by the Abbasids in the eighth century, on the banks of the Tigris River, Baghdad very quickly reached a dramatic level of commercial, cultural, and scientific development. Surrounded by a double ring of protective walls with four main gates, in its interior there appeared numerous stone buildings and beautifully decorated mosques, whose great domes proclaimed its magnificence.

Life in the City

As the main Muslim city under the Abbasid regime, Baghdad was in a state of constant activity. In its streets, craftsmen and traders mingled, as did settlers wanting to buy or sell.

ARCHITECTURE
Stone buildings of one or two floors burst onto the city landscape. Sellers and craftsmen sat around everywhere.

WATER
Needed for irrigation and personal use, water was one of the main preoccupations of Baghdad's inhabitants. Large wheels were made to extract water from lower levels so that it could be stored.

CARAVAN LEADERS
These had a distinctive presence within the city's environs. Their mules loaded with merchandise formed an incomparable attraction, and led eager buyers to gather.

CLOTHES
Ankle-length tunics and turbans were worn to combat the oppressive heat. They also added a splash of color to Baghdad's streets.

CHILDREN
Young children accompanied their mothers around the city. They did not all have formal schooling, except in religious matters.

SACRED ACTIVITY
Reading was a sacred activity for Muslims, since it was the means to learn the texts of the Koran. Moreover, scientific accomplishments led to new routes of interest and encouraged intellectual discussion.

CRAFTSMEN
The most varied articles could be found in Baghdad's markets and streets, where they were created within sight of passersby. It was the glassmakers who stood out among the craftsmen, creating pitchers, glasses, and bottles.

FISHING
One of the most important activities on the banks of the Tigris was fishing. It was not unusual to find patient fishermen seeking something different for the menu.

TEXTILES
Textiles were among Baghdad's most important products. Experts themselves in the art of dressmaking, the sellers exhibited their cloaks, fabrics, and rugs.

Sharing Living Quarters

The harem is a kind of matrimonial polygamy—that is, a union of more than two spouses. In the Muslim world, only a man is allowed to be united with more than one woman. During the ancient Ottoman Empire, in current Turkey, the harem was the area of the palace in which hundreds of women lived, including the wives, daughters, maids, and other female family members of the sultan. In the West, the harem is generally considered a place of amusement and personal satisfaction for powerful men. However, it was an area with strategic importance for the sultans, because they had to ensure that they would have descendants; and they could establish political alliances with the families of their wives.

All for One

Polygamy describes any kind of matrimony in which it is possible to have more than one spouse. However, there are two kinds of polygamy: polygyny and polyandry. Polygyny, in which one man can be married to more than one woman at the same time, was the kind practiced by the sultans in the ancient Ottoman Empire. Polyandry, which is much less common throughout the world, is when a woman can have two or more husbands simultaneously. The majority of men from societies where polygyny is allowed have only one wife. In the case of Muslims, this is because the Koran obliges them to give equal financial support to their wives. As a consequence, the custom of having several wives is usually limited to the richest and most powerful people. The fundamental dynamic of the sultan's harem was family politics. Descendants were of the utmost importance.

Family Orders

The Koran, the sacred book of the Islamic religion, allows a maximum of four wives per man, without exception.

A JUST HUSBAND
Islamic law obliges husbands to give a financial gift to their wives and let them manage it with complete liberty. Men must demonstrate generosity and respect.

Exclusive Territory of the Sultan

Sultans of the Ottoman Empire had absolute powers, and they were very careful about and jealous of all their wives. For that reason, the harem was a space where men were forbidden to enter, with the exception of eunuchs—men whose genitals had been mutilated—to avoid any objections or misunderstandings.

WATCHED OVER

By definition, a harem is a sanctuary or sacred area. Consequently, it was a strongly guarded space in which access, and the presence of any person not belonging there, was limited. The sultan provided clear and straightforward orders to the people who took care of his wives.

1

To the Sultan's Rhythm

The imperial harem was like that of any other powerful family, but more complex and extensive. The sultan could have four wives and an unlimited number of concubines. The sultan's young children could live there, as could his widowed mother, maiden sisters, and aunts.

1 **THE SULTAN**
Although he had ultimate authority in the palace, his conjugal relations had to follow a strict protocol.

2 **THE FIRST WIFE**
Bas haseki was the name given to the first wife and mother of the heir to the throne in the Ottoman Empire.

3 **OTHER WIVES**
They were called *haseki sultan*, which meant "mothers of the other children."

4 **MAIDS**
The harem also included female slaves in domestic service—a stable, trusted workforce.

5 **ODALISQUES**
Over time, the concept of a female slave who assisted the wives was generally extended to all women in the harem.

6 **EUNUCHS**
The word *eunuch* means "he who guards the women's beds." They were greatly trusted.

SUCCESSION
In the Ottoman Empire, the harem was an almost autonomous society, organized and hierarchical, in which all kinds of conspiracies could be plotted between rivals.

LIVING AMONG WOMEN
The function of the concubines was to give children to the master, while the female servants provided him with music, dance, and entertainment in general.

Reciting the Sacred Book

Islamic culture started expanding by the seventh century, shortly after Mohammed had begun to proclaim the new faith among the peoples of the Arabian Plateau. It is based on the belief in a single god, Allah, in his prophet Mohammed, and in his truths as revealed in the sacred book, the Koran, as well as a series of obligations with which all Muslims must comply. In the following centuries, its dominion spread over the southern and eastern Mediterranean, a good part of Eastern Europe, Asia, and all of Africa. Education, according to its precepts, occupied a central place in this civilization, with variations according to the different caliphs and viziers who held political power.

Readings and Prayers

During the Middle Ages, Islamic culture, with its scientific and literary knowledge, was dazzling. Classical culture was conserved, studied, and deepened. Muslim culture also excelled in arithmetic, geometry, algebra, natural sciences, and poetry. In accordance with Mohammed's teachings, all Muslims—men and women—had to know and recite the Koran, given that prayer was one of their sacred obligations. For this reason, elementary education was provided in the mosques, and it comprised reading, writing, and the basics in grammar and religion. Classes were based on memorizing the Koran—at least some parts of it— and on studying poetry. Some young people, between the ages of sixteen and twenty, undertook educational journeys that included visits to wise men and *imams*. These men gave free lessons in squares and other public spaces, including mosques and markets, on a variety of subjects, such as philosophy, grammar, logic, dialectics, theology, science, astronomy, jurisprudence, and dogmatics; they explained and recited the Koran, and instructed in the traditions.

Higher-level studies took place in the *madrasahs*, educational institutions typical of the Muslim world, where the Koran was studied in order to be memorized in its entirety.

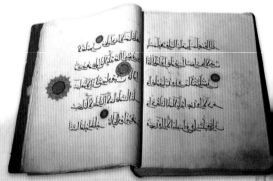

The Koran

The Muslims' sacred book is composed of 114 chapters, or *surahs*, consisting of a total of 6,236 verses called *ayat*.

The *Madrasahs*

Higher schools dedicated to the study of religious knowledge, the *madrasahs* tended to be near to or within a mosque. They included a prayer room and bedrooms for the pupils. They were founded for teaching the Koran, and then widened their scope to include language, law, Islamic law, history, music, medicine, mathematics, and astronomy. They were mostly for men, but there were also some for women.

1 GROUP READING
Every day, men gather in groups, in the open air, to read and recite the Koran.

2 FROM MEMORY
After learning to recite the complete Koran by heart, a title called *hafiz* is acquired.

3 LITERATE
Entry into the *madrasah* can be at any age, provided the pupil knows how to read and write.

4 ACCOMMODATION
The pupils study and live in individual bedrooms, where concentration and silence prevail.

5 ORPHANS
The *madrasahs* have a duty to accept as a pupil any orphan who requests teaching.

6 PUBLIC CLASSES
The wise men give public classes in squares and meeting places, always close to the mosques.

The Recitation

Reading the Koran also implies a special bodily position, in the method of sitting, of taking the book, and of reading it out loud.

Except for some very orthodox groups, the education of women is a very important matter within the Muslim culture.

SAMARKAND *MADRASAHS*
The *madrasahs* in Uzbekistan were very luxurious to reflect their importance and to honor Allah.

YEARS OF STUDY
Those people devoted to secular studies could spend twelve years in the *madrasah* before receiving the title of *ulema*.

ELEMENTARY EDUCATION
All Muslim children attended elementary school to learn the Koran.

Carrying the House on their Shoulders

At the start of the second millennium, numerous nomadic peoples still used dwellings that could be dismantled on their journeys. The Mongols, originating from the Central Asian steppes, used circular tents called yurts. They were protected with a thick roof, were easy to transport and were efficient in withstanding the extreme range of temperatures in the region. Each family had their own yurt, and visits from neighbors involved a rigorous protocol. Someone could be punished, even severely, simply for entering a leader's dwelling without announcing himself properly.

Constant Movement

For this kind of dwelling, the essential principle was its convenience in terms of pitching or dismantling. The Mongols covered long distances in adverse conditions, so they needed to be able to put up their tents easily and take them down immediately if circumstances required it.

1 INSIDE
The tents were austere inside. They had a low table, rugs for resting on, and trunks with personal objects and merchandise. A brazier was placed in the central area for cooking and keeping warm.

2 POWERFUL BEAMS
Wooden supports converged on a high central ring to hold the roof up. Force was exerted in a concentric manner, without the need to use posts inside the dwelling.

3 INTERNAL CURTAIN
Fabric or canvas was hung from the beams, at a certain distance from the walls. Its function was to separate the common space (situated in the center of the tent) from the private areas.

4 WALKING ON THE GROUND
The yurts were usually erected directly on the ground, although, in the case of well-to-do families, they were placed on wooden floors covered with rugs.

INGENUITY
There was only one wide door, which was enclosed by a frame of planks, tied to the central body of the tent by ropes.

STORAGE
The animals that they hunted, and the fruit they collected, were left inside the dwellings.

RING
The opening for ventilation and light on the upper side anchored the tension of the beams on which the roof was mounted.

EVOLUTION
In the past, yurts were designed so they could quickly be dismantled. However, nowadays they can be permanent and more modern materials are used.

COVERING
Depending on the season, the tents were covered with several layers of straw, thick woollen or fabric canvas, and ropes that could be tightened for securing them in place.

Step by Step

Some Mongol communities preserve the ancient traditions. To put up their houses, first, they mount the walls and the door frame. Then they put the roof beams in place with the central ring. Finally, they put the canvas covering in place.

FAMILY TIES

Nearby yurts generally belonged to members of the same clan. The position of each one was determined by blood ties.

LIVING TOGETHER

A strict code governed how the camps lived together. To avoid misunderstandings and conflicts between clans, guests had to announce themselves in advance.

Accelerated Expansion

The Mongols consisted of a federation of nomadic tribes, which, thanks to the yurts, could be easily mobilized across wide areas of the Asian continent. However, with the rise of their powerful leader, Genghis Khan, they managed successfully to settle down and consolidate an empire that challenged the centuries-old Chinese powers.

HANA
This was the Mongolian name for the walls. These consisted of a wooden framework, which served as support for the dwelling.

A Family Celebration

Festivals were one of the most vibrant and diverse recreational activities of the medieval period Chinese, who enjoyed get-togethers at home with their friends, relatives, and neighbors. With an abundance of food and rice wine, gatherings were livened up by acrobats and jugglers, and with firework displays and paper lanterns.

Family Relations

Elders had a special importance in Chinese family life, something that has changed little over time. A symbol of wisdom and levelheadedness, their central role in making important decisions prevailed, regardless of their economic power. During festivals, family relationships relaxed, abandoning the rigidity that normally dominated them.

A Garment for Festivities

The *chang-pao* is a long costume made from one piece of cloth worn by men as well as women. In common with all Chinese clothing, the material was loose and elaborately decorated with traditional motifs, such as the lotus flower and the dragon.

SERVICE

Food and drinks were served on a huge rug—slightly raised off the floor by a low platform. Fish, a variety of sauces, rice, camphor, and tea were some of the delicacies offered to the guests by large numbers of servants. The rice wine was kept in large vases and containers.

ACROBATICS

This was one of the most popular forms of entertainment in China. Jugglers and contortionists were prominent and amazed and amused those present with their skills.

RIBBONS

At occasions involving collective entertainment, women displayed considerable dexterity, especially in their ribbon dances. They were generally admired for the precision of the movements and the beautiful shapes they created.

ELEGANT TABLEWARE

The delicate pieces of porcelain that the Chinese produced under the Yuan dynasty were famed for their fine white-and-blue cobalt decoration. The porcelain industry, promoted at that time, was exceptional because of its extraordinary glazes. On the left is a Yuan plate from the fourteenth century with a drawing of a fish.

Japanese Houses

Japanese houses at this time provided a core feature for their occupants, namely practicality. The materials used in their construction allowed certain changes in their internal layouts; for example, to extend the rooms according to requirements. That same practicality governed the choice of predominantly light materials. Wood and paper were preferred, although tiles, straw, and occasionally stone were also used.

THE TRADITIONAL *MINKA*

The most popular houses in Japan, which originated in the feudal period, were called *minkas*, and their structure and materials varied according to the climatic conditions of the region. Among their main features, their practical design stands out, as does the uniqueness of the building components, whose lightness is associated with a certain philosophy of life itself. In this sense, for the Japanese a garden or a fountain is more important than the solidity of their walls.

The Family Buddhist Altar

In accordance with the high spirituality preached and practiced in each sphere of their daily lives, almost all traditional Japanese homes still to this day have their own Buddhist altar, whose dimensions vary according to the available space.

The altar is presided over by the figure of Buddha, whose image can be repeated in his different representations.

THE HEARTH

The fire was generally kept lit and was the main source of heat for the home. It was occasionally used for cooking.

THE *DOMA*

This area was covered with wood and, with its floor of flattened earth, was the place where inhabitants took off their shoes.

EXTERNAL SPACE

Called *engawa*, this area was like a roofed balcony or veranda in form. Covered with wood, it also served as the main entrance for guests, who took off their shoes on a stone slab, which is usually at one side.

LINTELS
Made of wood and profusely decorated with engravings, these served to show the boundaries of each room.

LOFTS
Part of almost all the nobles' houses, these tended to be used for storing a very diverse set of objects and merchandise.

ROOFS
The roof could take a number of forms and be made from a variety of materials. They were normally pitched, with tiles on a wooden framework. Occasionally, the tiles ended in a striking decoration. There were also straw roofs and small wooden boards.

SLIDING DOORS
These moved from one side to the other to allow the room to be made larger in the desired direction.

VERTICAL POSTS
These were introduced into the foundations to reduce humidity inside. In addition, if placed symmetrically, they gave solidity to the whole.

TATAMIS
These mats made from straw and reeds covered the floors in the nobles' rooms. Because their measurements were standardized, they sometimes serve to give an exact idea of the size of the room—generally from six to eight mats.

Attuned to the Environment

*H*anok is the name given to traditional Korean houses. From the outset, they were created as environmentally friendly dwellings made from various raw materials, for example, wood, stone, mud, and paper. In the past, they were distinguished by their roofs; tiles were confined to powerful Koreans, while the common people had straw roofing. The architectural styles of these dwellings were also adapted to the different climates: in the cold north, protection against the winds was the priority; in the warmer south, freely circulating air was preferred.

A Warm Home

Because the *Hanok* structure is made of wood, it favors the creation of very warm, welcoming rooms. The outside covering is made of bricks prepared from a mixture of soil and grass, and the floor is made of stone and soil. *Hanji*, traditional Korean paper, is of special importance for these constructions. It is used for covering windows, walls, and doors. On completion, it is also put on the floors, after a process of oiling. The *ondol*, or heating system, is a distinguishing feature.

WIDENING THE SURFACE
The yard surrounding the home allows for easy movement around the whole perimeter. The north end enables the breeze to enter.

RESPECTING THE LANDSCAPE
Korean architecture takes into account homes' natural surroundings. The principle, known as *baesanimsu*, implies that the ideal house should be built with a river in front and a mountain behind.

ADAPTING TO NECESSITY
The layout of the floors can vary, depending on the area. In the warm south, they are L-shaped to encourage ventilation. In the cold north, they form a "U" or a square to conserve the temperature.

CAREFULLY CONSIDERED
Roofs extend farther out than the walls to protect the sides of the house from rain. Windows and doors are elegantly decorated, and at low cost, with *hanji*. Nowadays glass is also included.

A Touch of Distinction

It is usually said that the windows and doors of the *hanok* are the most important parts of the dwelling. Richly ornamented, they have numerous poles with distinctive decorative motifs, called *di-sal*. Inside, wood and paper are highly regarded as construction materials.

1 ROOF
Tile-roofed houses are called *kiwajip*. Straw-thatched houses are called *chogajip*, and, although more economical, have in recent times fallen into disuse.

2 HEART OF THE HOME
The open central courtyard is what articulates the space. Around this are the rooms and the elevated galleries—a setting for social exchange and family rest.

3 OUTBUILDINGS
In the past, the bathrooms and kitchen were found in separate buildings, away from the *hanok* itself. Now, these rooms can be located inside the home, with better access and greater comfort.

4 CUSTOMS
The bedrooms tend to be small in order to preserve the heat, given that beds are made up on the floor. Nowadays, new technologies are included, alongside traditional methods, in order to improve home comforts.

Perimeter of the dwelling

Side courtyard

Original Heating

The *ondol* is a typical Korean heating system, cleverly designed by means of subterranean pipes. On lighting the fire in the lower end of the kitchen, the surface of the dwelling is heated evenly and economically.

ELEVATION
The construction, based around a courtyard, is built very high above ground. This is because these dwellings have a heating system in the ground that covers the whole area.

Ventilation chimney

Main entrance

Asian Warriors

The vast Asiatic territory witnessed a huge range of changes during the Middle Ages: the rising of new empires and the decline of others, the formation of federations of kingdoms, as well as the existence of feudal states. They all had armies of the most diverse kind that frequently ended up confronting one another. From soldiers of the different Chinese dynasties to brave Korean warriors, from the famous Samurai to the Mongol conquerors—each was formidable in its own way, with unique characteristics very different to those of their counterparts in the West.

The Three Kingdoms

The years AD 57 and 668 were known as the period of the Three Kingdoms in Korea. Goguryeo (the largest of the three), Baekje, and Silla were the names of the kingdoms that dominated the greater part of the Korean Peninsula during a substantial part of the first millennium. Goguryeo occupied the south of what is currently Manchuria, the areas to the north and center of the Korean Peninsula, and south of Primorsky in what is currently Russia. It was one of the most important and powerful states of Eastern Asia, and its expansionist politics inevitably led it to clash with China at different periods. The war with the Wei dynasty (244–245) almost culminated in the disappearance of Goguryeo, whose capital was destroyed, and it had to be raised

from the ashes. A new conflict broke out 250 years later, this time with the Sui dynasty, which in 589 had unified China after four centuries of division. The kingdom of Goguryeo had become an important regional power, thanks to King Gwanggeto the Great's wars of expansion. For the Sui, Goguryeo was a threat that had to be eliminated. They launched various campaigns to try to conquer it in the years 598, 612, 613, and 614, all of which failed. The most disastrous campaign was that of 612—the critical landmark battle of Salsu, considered the most bloody in world history.

Samurai

Characteristic warriors of medieval Japan, Samurai were experts in the use of the sword (*katana*), the bow and the horse.

Chinese and Mongols

In March 1974, in the Chinese province of Shaanxi, a formidable model army—of almost 7,000 soldiers—on a life-size scale, with their terra-cotta horses and carts, was discovered (*see left*). The terra-cotta army belonged to the Quin dynasty, and provides a great example of how the Chinese imperial armies must have looked.

GENGHIS KHAN

In the thirteenth century, under the leadership of Genghis Khan (*right*), the Mongols created the second major empire in history, governing more than 100 million people over 13.5 million square miles (35 million square kilometers). They achieved this on account of their army, which made a religion out of mobility and logistics.

DECIMAL SYSTEM

One of Genghis Khan's innovations was the use of the decimal system in his army: each group of troops was formed in different multiples of ten. Moreover, he created a great network of messengers for sending out his orders, and established logistics officials for supplying substitute horses and equipment.

Battle of Salsu

In the year 612 the Chinese emperor Yahgdi invaded Goguryeo at the head of an army of 1,133,800 men. One portion of these troops, the Left Army, was ambushed by the Goguryeo soldiers at the river Salsu, and 302,300 men were killed, out of a total of 305,000 soldiers.

Chinese Army

This was a large and well-armed, but unsuccessful in its attempt to take the capital of Goguryeo.

Korean Soldiers

Although they had an infantry (*left*) and archers (*right*), the Goguryeo army excelled because of its excellent cavalry (*center*), which was decisive at the battle of Salsu.

Trapped in the River

The Left Army tried to take the capital of Goguryeo, without success. When the Chinese withdrew, crossing the relatively dry bed of the Salsu River, General Eulji Mundeok ordered his men to knock down the dam that contained its water.

WITHOUT PITY
The Goguryeo cavalry ambushed the survivors at the riverbanks.

FEW SURVIVED
There was outright victory. Only around 2,700 Chinese managed to survive.

LETHAL WATERS
Hundreds of thousands of Chinese soldiers drowned.

From the Far East to the World

While the West was still in the Middle Ages and suffering from the advance of the Black Death, the East became the most progressive region in the world: it was the most populated, the most productive, and had achieved the greatest scientific and technological development. Protected by their emperors, the Chinese, Korean, and Japanese researchers created all kinds of inventions that, only centuries later, would arrive in Europe. For example, by the first century, the Chinese already manufactured paper, they used gunpowder, and they had used a compass since the fourth century BC. They also invented matches (sixth century), porcelain (seventh century), the mechanical clock (eighth century), playing cards (ninth century), phosphorescent painting, and even the roller chain (tenth century).

Pioneering Wisdom

It is estimated that more than half of the inventions and basic discoveries upon which the modern world relies originated in China. If that society had not developed the compass, for example, Christopher Columbus would not have arrived in the Americas. In its first periods of expansion, China's bureaucratic feudalism favored science to an extraordinary extent. The Chinese were pioneers in the production of cast iron. They invented the suspension bridge, and constructed chain bridges with cast-iron chain links. Also, thanks to their advanced metallurgic industry, in the third century AD, they started to manufacture smelted iron and bronze supports. They already knew about the decimal system (fourteenth century BC), negative numbers, fractions, and the value of pi, formulated by Liu Hui in the year 260. Advances in Japan and Korea were somewhat overshadowed by the enormous scientific and technological contribution from the Chinese.

Jomon Ceramics

The most ancient pottery in the world derives its name from the period of Japanese culture lasting from 14,000 BC to 300 BC. The clay was decorated by cutting grooves in it or by pressing into its surface with rope.

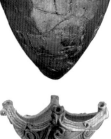

Korean Inventions

Jang Yeong-sil, a scientist and astronomer who lived in the fifteenth century during the Joseon dynasty, was one of the most important inventors in the Far East. Among his creations was a series of sun clocks situated at principal locations in Seoul, so that the people could check the time.

EARTHQUAKE DETECTOR

The world's first seismograph was called Houfeng Didong Yi and was built by the scientist Zhang Heng around the year AD 130. It consisted of six balls balanced in a bronze vessel.

Flow of Time

Su Song, a government employee and engineer, constructed this Chinese astronomical water clock in 1088. The major components had been smelted in bronze, while the timber tower that housed it measured 20 feet (6 meters).

1 ARMILLARY SPHERE
In the upper part was a bronze sphere, in whose interior a ringed globe rotated automatically, which displayed the position of the celestial bodies.

2 WATER TANKS
A conduit provided running water; a stream of water poured from a water tank onto the blades of a wheel, which would start to rotate.

WORKERS
Because of its size, the tower needed several operators.

3 THE TIME
The mechanism caused little figures to appear, which indicated the time, the lunar cycles, and the motion of the firmament.

4 DRAINAGE
The construction also held a residual container for water leaks.

SU SONG
As well as his invention, he made contributions in other areas, including in astronomy, cartography, and botany.

ACTIVATION
The mechanism always required the same quantity of water to function.

DESTRUCTION
The clock was destroyed by the Tartars in the twelfth century, during their invasion of China.

The Americas

W. Langdon Kihn '41

The Americas were first inhabited by nomadic tribes from Asia, who crossed the frozen Bering Strait into what is modern-day Alaska some time around 20,000 BC. These tribes spread out, reaching Cape Horn about 10,000 years later, and went on to establish civilizations such as the

Maya, the Aztec, and the Inca. Meanwhile, indigenous cultures we now call Native Americans settled on the central plains of North America. In 1492, Christopher Columbus, under the aegis of the Spanish crown, landed on the Caribbean island of Hispaniola, ushering in the extensive European colonization of the continents.

Mayan Dwellings

Mayan peasant houses were not all the same shape, although the floors were mainly rectangular and oval. In general, mud and reeds were used for the walls and straw for the roof. The floors were of rolled earth. As in almost all pre-Hispanic cultures, furniture was scant, and ventilation and light coming through the windows was almost nonexistent. The women did all the chores in the home.

FARMING

It was common for small fields to be cultivated on one side of the dwelling. On these were grown corn or beans—the basis of the family group's food. The head of the family worked in these fields, accompanied by his sons.

Preparing Food

One of the main tasks for Mayan women was preparing daily meals for the whole family, for which they ground grain in large mortars. They also placed a portion of the milled grain into pots for storage.

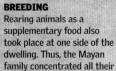

BREEDING

Rearing animals as a supplementary food also took place at one side of the dwelling. Thus, the Mayan family concentrated all their activities in a small area.

The Mayan "kitchen" was completed by a group of ceramic pots, generally placed around a mortar.

FURNITURE
This was scant. They slept on a bed of poles covered with cotton blankets. Hammocks were also frequently used.

THE ROOF
This was built from palm leaves and straw. It was generally high, and pitched, or with a pyramidal shape, and held up by a wooden frame.

THE KITCHEN
Occupying a central place in the dwelling. It consisted of a small cleft for the fire.

WORK
The work carried out by women was usually done in their own house. Not only did they prepare the daily meals there and store food, but they also made the family's clothing.

BUILDING MATERIALS
These varied according to the region and period. Generally, houses with reed and mud walls were the most common.

Strength through Union

Everyday life in Inca society took place within communities called *ayllu*. Daily tasks were organized collectively and were directed, on the one hand, toward mutual collaboration between families and, on the other, to responding to the demands of the state. The formation of a new family nucleus was the way to attain adulthood and full recognition within the community. If a couple passed the *servinakuy*, an advanced matrimonial test to establish their compatibility, a definitive and indissoluble conjugal union was consecrated. Members of the *ayllu* helped in building the new home and supplied the necessary tools.

Communal Life

The *ayllu* was a community of peasants united by family ties, who had ancestors in common and lived in the same territory. The family institution was so important that a person was not considered an adult before contracting a formal union. Within these cultural parameters, it could be expected that males would get married at the age of twenty-four or older and women from the age of eighteen. If a man was unable to find a wife on his own, the state took charge, offering him a group of women to choose from.

Inca society was ruled by two principles: reciprocity and redistribution. Reciprocity governed relations between members of the communities, and included the need for permanent mutual assistance. Redistribution referred to the food and supplies that any community might need. This was administered by the state, whose highest authority was the Inca.

The state handed over land to each community for its subsistence, and, annually, a local official assigned plots to each family according to the number of family members. The peasants did not own the land and the plots were worked collectively by the whole community.

THE ROYAL COUPLE

The principal wife of the Inca was his sister. Only the monarch could be joined in marriage to more than one woman.

THE INCA

The Inca was monarch of divine origin, and supreme authority in the empire.

Populating the World

According to old tales, the Sun god, or *Inti*, gave life to the first mortals at Lake Titicaca, so that they could populate the world. He entrusted the four Ayar brothers and their sister-wives to initiate the Inca family. Ayar Manco and Mama Ocilo were the first royal couple and they founded Cuzco.

The Making of a New Home

When a couple were joined in marriage, the entire family community helped to build the new dwelling. The state also gave them support: it handed over a portion of land to the couple for them to maintain, and every time a child was born, it handed over more land.

1 NEOLOCAL
Married couples moved to a new independent residence separate from their families.

2 WEAVING FOR EVERYONE
Spinning was one of the main activities for mothers and young girls.

3 SHARING FOOD
Potatoes and corn grown in the *ayllu* were shared equally among the families.

4 HELPING AT HOME
Boys cared for the animals and girls helped with the domestic chores in the home.

5 LIVESTOCK
Llama and alpaca breeding was an important activity in the Inca economy.

Fertile Land

Farming on terraces increased the arable surface area on the hillsides in the mountain ranges.

Nomadic Skills

The tepee, used mainly by indigenous cultures on the central plains of North America, is one of the best-designed camping homes in terms of its habitability, comfort, and adaptation to extreme weather conditions. It became the normal form of abode among the nomadic tribes of the prairies. It allowed its inhabitants to live in a harsh climate, providing a warm home in winter and a cool one in summer.

From Experience

The tepee is seen as a vernacular dwelling, because it is an expression of an ancestral tradition in construction and because it uses indigenous materials that are returned to nature without the risk of environmental pollution when no longer needed. This kind of tent was created by the original inhabitants on the North American prairies, based on their ancestral knowledge—that is, it developed from the experience of previous generations. One of the main aims of this kind of shelter was to achieve a microclimate on the inside in order to attain a certain degree of comfort and minimize the harshness of extreme climates. These homes were built with disposable materials from the surrounding area.

SIZE
The smallest tepees were 7 feet (2 meters) in diameter; the largest reached 40 feet (12 meters).

Mystic Symbols

Each part of the tepee had symbolic meanings. The tent floor represented mother earth, the roof, father sky; each pole symbolized the journey between man and the spiritual world. The outside space was the domain of creator fathers. Even its orientation, toward the east, came from the hope of being awoken by the sun, the generator of life.

1 SHELTER
In winter, bonfires were lit inside the tents for cooking food and helping to cope with low temperatures.

HUNTING MATERIALS
Properly treated buffalo skin was used for wrapping a frame of posts, which were polished to avoid injury.

3 DECORATION
It was the custom for each family to decorate the inside of the tepee with rugs and textiles made by the women of the group.

2 STRENGTH
Because of their conical shape, the crisscross arrangement of posts provided a resistant, stable structure, even in strong winds.

4 COMMUNITY
The ancestral ties that united the people were always present. In summer, there were community bonfires in the open air.

ANNOUNCING ARRIVAL
If the door was open, it was the custom that everyone was free to enter; but if it was shut, it was of vital importance to call and wait until those inside authorized entry.

ABLE TO BE DISMANTLED
The tepee could be erected or dismantled in less than two hours, even by women or children. All the materials were transported, and they adapted to any climate.

Living on Water

Built on piles or stakes, stilt houses are dwellings erected over diverse water surfaces around the world. They can be found on lakes, lagoons, rivers, marshy ground, and by the sea. This particular architectural concept dates from the Neolithic period, and is a remarkable example of a building adapted to its surroundings. The construction materials are indigenous—that is, they are provided by the natural conditions close by. The abundance of aquatic environments ensures the provision of water supplies and communication routes. As would be expected, fishing is the main economic activity.

Across the Globe

Spread across all continents, this kind of dwelling can be found in diverse places that are very different from each other. A model can be found in Venezuela, where the Warao community built these houses on the delta of the Orinoco River.

1 LET IT DRIP
The roof slope stops leaks and allows a rapid clearing of water from tropical storms.

2 BASKETWORK
The rushes from the riverbanks supply the raw material for making baskets and containers, which can be used for storing food.

3 IN CONTACT
The dwellings usually have communicating bridges and walkways. A boat made from logs provides each dwelling with independent access to the river.

TO WORK
Water erosion is constant, which means it is necessary to continuously carry out maintenance tasks.

Moriche Palm

This is a species of palm tree, native to Central America. Fibers are extracted from its leaves, which can be used for making mooring ropes to secure the stilt-house structures. Its fruit, rich in protein, is used for making oil and highly nutritious food products.

TRANSPORTATION
Boats are used as transportation in stilt-house communities.

SIESTA
Hammocks or small mats designed for resting are made with vegetable fabrics or fibers typical of each region.

Neolithic Origin

In about 2000 BC, in the Bronze Age, stilt houses became more stable dwellings thanks to the use of axes, which could fell trees larger than 6 inches (15 centimeters) in diameter. Earlier, in the Stone Age, builders stacked stones and trunks around the piles to stop them from sinking into ground that was less resistant.

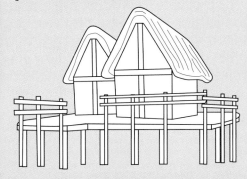

ADVANTAGES
These constructions, erected above the water, allow the dwellings to be kept clean and protected from wild animals. At the same time, they also leave a larger surface area for ground dedicated to farming activities.

AGAINST HUMIDITY
The scant walls allow air to circulate to counteract the humidity of the environment. The fire and hearth, which are inside, strengthen this effect. It is customary to place them close to the water on stones and clay.

THE PILES
The houses are constructed on wooden stakes and oriented according to the prevailing winds. In the case of the Warao dwellings, the piles are made from mangroves. In some places—such as Santa Rosa de Agua, on Lake Maracaibo—they include concrete piles and sheets of boarding, which are more resistant but not so easily renewable.

Transatlantic Foods

The arrival of Europeans in the Americas initiated one of the most significant transformations ever in global eating habits. In the first years of the conquest, early Spanish resistance to consuming products from American territory led to plants and animals being transported from the Old World to the New. To appease the Crown for a while, given the difficulties in finding the precious metals that it desired, the Spanish tried to send the authorities any exotic foods that the indigenous people offered them. Gradually, the flow of products in both directions, between the Old World and the New, transformed the flora and fauna, and notably enriched the diet of the inhabitants in both regions.

Trying the Exotic

At the start, the conquistadors scorned indigenous food and continued to eat the basic products carried in their boats: wheat, wine, salted fish, vegetables, and fruit. The American population did not benefit immediately from these goods, because they were consumed exclusively by Spaniards. However, slowly, the plants and animals brought from Europe adapted successfully to the different climates, and started to be incorporated in American diets. The Europeans brought numerous species of animals. Cattle multiplied in the wild, goats were used for their meat and milk, and sheep were exploited both for eating and for their wool, which was used for weaving. Finally, pigs arrived, which were kept in farmyards and whose number expanded the most rapidly. Horses, mules, and donkeys frightened the first indigenous people who saw them, but they became established as beasts of burden and were used for transportation. Among the poultry, the most widespread was the hen for the tastiness of its eggs and meat. Most of the American contributions were of a vegetable nature, such as corn, tomato, pumpkin, cocoa, and vanilla. The animal with the most impact on the European diet was the turkey, weighing 22–35 pounds (10–15 kilograms), from which they used the meat and eggs as well as the feathers for decorations and crafts.

Dog Meat

The xoloitzcuintli is a breed of dog without hair, originating in Mesoamerica. Its meat was used as food, and the animal was usually sold alive in the city markets. It was also valued in rituals, such as ball games, and in homes as a pet.

XOLOTL
Mexican god
represented as a dog.

The Impact of Cattle

The encounter between Europeans and Americans was traumatic and surprising. Both peoples experienced equally the impact of physical and cultural differences and different foods. The conquistadors brought numerous domesticated animals that integrated easily into the geographical diversity and culinary traditions of the New World.

1 HORSES
The main breed of horse that the Spanish brought to the Americas was a cross between an Andalusian stallion and a Quarter Horse mare. Its coat was a dark chestnut color.

2 ANIMAL TRILOGY
Pigs, sheep, and goats formed the "animal trilogy" of the Spanish conquest. Pigs multiplied rapidly and were well accepted. Cattle took longer to become widespread.

3 XOLOITZCUINTLI
The name comes from the Nahuatl language; it is considered to be one of the oldest purebreeds of dog in existence. Its archaeological remains date from more than 3,000 years ago.

4 GUAJOLOTES
This is a species of turkey, domesticated by the Aztecs for consumption and the laying of eggs. It can reach 4 feet (1.10 meters) in length, with the breadth of its wings measuring 5 feet (1.44 meters).

PALM TREES
They provided palm hearts and coconuts—exotic products for European tastes.

Aztec Dwellings

Aztec houses had a rectangular ground plan, which differed according to the social class of the occupants. The main construction materials were clay, wood, and straw for the peasants' houses, and stone for the ruling classes and those living in towns. The former were small and were illuminated by torches; the latter had rooms set around one or more courtyards. The furniture was scant or totally nonexistent, except in the royal palaces and nobles' houses. Constructed beside these dwellings, the steam baths were a remarkable adjunct: the stone walls were heated externally until red hot, at which point the individual, on entering, threw water onto them to produce huge quantities of steam.

FOOD
Baskets were placed around the houses for corn, sweet potatoes, tomatoes, and other produce, which were used for making meals.

THE MEN
Most of the work relating to agricultural production and fishing was carried out by men. Excess produce was transferred to large baskets and kept in communal storerooms.

NETS
Held up by poles submerged in the lake, nets served as traps for ducks and geese, which were part of the family diet.

ARTIFICIAL ISLANDS

Dwellings were constructed near these small floating islands called *chinampas*, which were used for farming. They were constructed on lakes, and families worked on them to meet the requirements for their own subsistence as well as those of the ruling nobility. The tools and implements necessary for the work were kept either in their own houses or outside.

ROOF
The roof could be flat or sloping, and was constructed entirely from thick layers of overlaid straw held up by a wooden frame.

WALLS
The houses were made from clay and could have one or two rooms, separated by curtains of cloth or rush matting. The most lowly dwellings lacked windows and had only one entrance.

WOMEN
Women carried out the domestic tasks, which included cleaning the house, making clothes, and preparing meals.

BLANKETS
Blankets, skins and rush matting were used for sleeping on. They rested directly on the earthen floor. The better-off families usually had floors of mortar or polished stone.

GRINDING STONE
Women prepared meals by grinding corn on a slightly concave rectangular stone called a *metate*.

GRILL
The dwellings had an oval clay grill known as a *comal*, on which corn snacks were toasted. The embers were placed on the floor below the grill, and between the stones which supported it.

Two Classes of School

The Aztec Empire dominated a substantial part of current Mexican territory between the fourteenth century and the Spanish conquest. They were a warrior people who had established a theocratic system and a complex society. They developed forms of writing, achieved mathematical and astrological supremacy, and erected magnificent architectural structures. The worship of ancestors and gods, and the production of warriors, guided their educational practices. Classes were given in the *calmecac* and in the *telpochcalli*.

Government Training

An institution known as the *calmecac*, which in Nahuatl means "row of houses," was responsible for preparing pupils to carry out government activities, based on discipline, work, and dedication. The children of nobles were trained for the priesthood here. They studied arts, such as dance and painting, and sciences, such as mathematics and astronomy. The teaching was fundamentally religious, despite the fact that many of the students did not intend to become priests and were trained for jobs in the military or with the authorities.

Before entering, it was necessary to have attended the so-called "House of Strength," where they were instructed in basic military skills. Parents committed their children to the priesthood as soon as they were born. Between the ages of seven and fifteen, they were offered by their parents to the leaders of the *calmecac*, who would be invited to a banquet. The children were then taken to the temple, where they were painted black and given a collar with wooden beads called a *tlacopatli*. This confirmed their entry into the school and their membership of that institution, where they would become boarders.

Sporting Practices

Ball games, in which a rubber ball must enter through a stone hoop, were practiced in *telpochcalli* and had a ritual function. The result was understood to predict the future.

Master Priest

The teachers at the *calmecac* were priests, and used several forms of physical punishment as a favored educational tool.

LESSONS
Songs based on verses and prayers that expressed the duties of individuals were sung.

PUPILS
They learned to write on the *amate* paper, drawing the codices using paintbrushes and red, blue, and yellow inks.

PRINCIPAL PRIESTS
To become a priest of the White Order of Quetzalcoatl involved approximately fifteen years of training in the *calmecac*.

Warrior School

Dedicated to the male population, an institution called the *telpochcalli* encouraged men to become warriors and to serve the community. Pupils entered at the age of fifteen, accompanied by their parents. They had to do jobs, such as repairing the temples and collectively working the land.

CEREMONIES

There were ceremonies dedicated to Quetzalcoatl, the creator god, and Huitzilapochtli, god of war.

DISCIPLINE

Life in the *telpochcalli* was very hard and demanding. It started each morning with a cold water bath, and the food was frugal and rationed.

1 EDUCATORS
The teachers were already trained as priests and warriors; they were distinguished in the sphere of the *telpochcalli* by their clothes, trimmings, and accessories.

3 OTHER TASKS
As well as being trained for war and games, boys were educated in ritual dances, poetry, song, sciences, and technology.

5 WEAPONS FOR TRAINING
For combat training, they used arms like the *macuahuitl*— a wooden sword with obsidian blades.

2 UNTIL ADULTHOOD
Training finished at twenty years old, at which point the students were regarded as warriors. Then they could get married and return to their homes.

4 LOCATION
There was a *telpochcalli* in each district of the Aztec Empire situated in the vicinity of a temple.

6 LOWER CLASS
The *macehualtin*—Aztecs of low social class—went to the warrior school.

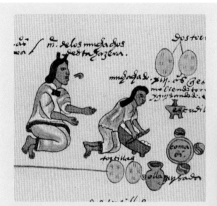

Female Education

The training of Aztec women was mainly carried out by their mothers at home. They were taught religion, cooking, and various techniques, such as farming and how to use a loom.

IDENTIFYING SIGNS
A distinguishing mark, such as a stone embedded in the lip, verified that someone belonged to the *telpochcalli*.

3 EARLY MODERN AND MODERN HISTORY

162

172

Early Modern and Modern History

The early modern period in Europe saw the flowering of education, arts, and science. As advances in trade and travel brought continents together, landscapes, ways of life, and human understanding of the world were transformed. In the late eighteenth century, industrialization was the springboard that took people from living in sparsely populated, largely rural areas to the crowded, busy, high-tech cities of the twenty-first century, with global economies, instant communication, and travel that extended not only all around the world but also into space.

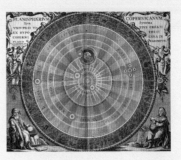

1543
COPERNICAN THEORY

Nicolaus Copernicus revolutionized astronomy and philosophical thought with his theory of heliocentrism (left). He affirmed that the earth is not the center of the cosmos: it revolves around the sun, and not the other way around.

1825
RAILROADS

The invention of steam trains revolutionized transportation, speeding up travel and linking towns and villages like never before. This had a huge impact on industry, which was no longer restricted to transporting large quantities of goods by water.

1850
CHILD LABOR

Children were a key part of the workforce during the Industrial Revolution and suffered terribly from the poor conditions, long working hours, and low pay. They were commonly used by the textile industry, because their small hands were ideal for operating the machinery of the time.

1890
UNDERGROUND

The City and South London Railway began to operate in December 1890, heralding a new era in urban transportation. Subway systems became an indispensable means of transportation in major cities across the world.

1903
FLYING

With the invention of the airplane, traveling long distances became much faster, but came at a high price.

1961
HUMANS IN SPACE

Russian cosmonaut Yuri Gagarin (left) became the first human being to travel in space. His complete orbit of the planet at a height of 186 miles (300 kilometers) saw the beginning of the age of manned space flights.

1969
APOLLO XI

On July 20, 1969, U.S. astronaut Neil Armstrong, commander of the Apollo XI mission, became the first human being to set foot on the moon.

1980s Onward
INFORMATION TECHNOLOGY

From the 1980s onward, the way we work (and the way we play) has been revolutionized by the popularization and wide distribution of computers and the internet.

1633
GALILEO CONDEMNED

The Florentine astronomer and physicist Galileo (right), was the first person to use a telescope to look at the sky. He attempted to convince ecclesiastical skeptics of heliocentrism, but the ecclesiastical hierarchy did not accept his ideas and condemned him for heresy in 1633.

Eighteenth Century
THE ABOLITION OF SLAVERY

It is estimated that twenty million Africans were enslaved and transported to the American colonies during the almost four centuries that the slave trade lasted. Starting from the eighteenth century, abolitionist movements ended this sinister practice.

Eighteenth Century
MIGRATION TO THE CITIES

Industrialization prompted huge numbers of people to migrate from rural areas to the cities in search of factory jobs.

1852
DEPARTMENT STORES

Bon Marché, the world's first department store, opened in Paris in 1852. Having one store housed in a large building of several stories and divided into sections, or departments, offered a completely new shopping experience.

1868
THE TYPEWRITER

Christopher Sholes's invention of the typewriter met with commercial success. Production of the technology was standardized in the early twentieth century.

Late Nineteenth Century
THE SCHOOLMISTRESS IN CONTROL

Elementary school education became compulsory across many countries in the late nineteenth century. Literacy began to spread among the masses as education was declared a basic right.

Early Twentieth Century
SKYSCRAPERS

The invention of the elevator in the mid-nineteenth century was crucial to the development of skyscrapers. By the early twentieth century, many city landscapes around the world had been transformed with high-rise buildings.

1931
EMPIRE STATE BUILDING

Inaugurated in 1931, this iconic 365,000-ton, 102-story structure (right) held the title of the world's tallest building for four decades.

1957
SPUTNIK

The first artificial satellite in history was launched into space by the Soviets in October 1957. Sputnik II followed a month later, and was sent into orbit with Laika, a dog, as its crew.

2008
GLOBAL FINANCIAL CRISIS

Among the effects of the global financial crisis that erupted in 2008 were huge fluctuations in the value of commodities. Demand slowed down, investors were discouraged, and many products struggled to recover their value.

And beyond
SPACE TOURISM

SpaceShipTwo will be the first vessel to take tourists into space. It will travel about 68 miles (110 km) from the earth's surface so tourists will have the possibility of experiencing microgravity for a few minutes.

The Early Modern Period

L asting from the late sixteenth century to the early eighteenth century, the early modern period is marked by its transitional nature and featured numerous events and intellectual movements that have had a lasting influence on modern society: the scientific and technological

imperatives, secular civil politics, and capitalist economics—these were all cast in the crucible of emergent nation states where artistic and cultural movements were also beginning to thrive. It was also an era of geographical exploration, notable for the rise and decline of the first global empires.

Reevaluating the Past

During the Renaissance, the fifteenth and sixteenth centuries, a cultural movement developed that expanded through the central regions of Europe, especially the Italian cities. The various artistic currents aimed to recover the appearance and harmony of Greco-Roman antiquity, and there was a return to using straight lines, columns, and domes in architecture. The wealthier sectors of society, such as the leading merchants, began to live in houses that reflected the resurgence of these styles. These were homes with several floors that housed the close family, the extended family, and the servants. Many also included areas for work, commercial premises, and offices.

The Dwelling as Home

The dwelling acquired enormous importance, becoming the center of social life. The expansion of interregional trade led to businesses being incorporated into everyday life.

MATERIALS USED
The basic materials used in the construction of houses were wood and stone.

COMBINED STYLES
The architecture of straight lines and tall constructions coexisted with the arches of classicism. The arched access door was a common feature.

The Rural Villa

The wealthy owned exclusive country residences. Villa Capra, by the Italian Andrea Palladio, is one of the best examples of this type of construction.

TALL WINDOWS
Large windows illuminated and ventilated the central rooms.

1 **BUSINESS AT HOME**
Family businesses usually operated on the first floor. They were housed in the rooms that faced onto the street and remained open throughout the day.

2 THE KITCHEN
The Renaissance kitchen was usually located on the top floor. It was far from the main hall and the side room to keep away smells and noise.

3 PLACE OF CELEBRATION
The main hall was the largest room in the house. It was here that visitors were received and the most important family celebrations, such as weddings, were held.

4 MULTIPURPOSE MAIN BEDROOM
The side room was not only used for sleeping. It was also the meeting place of the nuclear family—that is, the private space of parents and children.

5 LIGHTING
The rooms had diffused lighting, because, generally, wax paper was used to cover the windows. Glass windows were rare and were only found in luxury dwellings.

COLONNADES
Colonnades were inspired by the palaces and temples of Greco-Roman antiquity.

COURTYARD
The main rooms faced onto this open, internal space, permitting a certain privacy.

Setting Boundaries

The development of mercantile activities and the growth in European cities led to changes in the organization of the home. Medieval extended families began to give way to restricted patriarchal families—smaller, confined, and of an urban character. Gradually, the notions of intimacy and individualism, in a modern sense, spread among the privileged groups and, later, reached the people as a whole. Between the sixteenth and eighteenth centuries, families broke the links of mutually dependent solidarity with the community, distanced themselves from ancestral bonds, and strong traditional ties of kinship disappeared.

Stage of Transition

Some specialists used the concept of "restricted patriarchal family" to refer to the model of union that began to develop in the upper strata of European society from the early sixteenth to the early eighteen century. The trends toward greater privacy, the female role as "housewife," and the paternal role as the economic provider for the family were slowly imposed by these privileged sectors and gave rise to the nuclear family, which became consolidated after the Industrial Revolution in the West. This phase of family development was associated with an increasing emphasis on the importance of love between the married couple, although there was also an increase in the authoritarian power of fathers. Family roles were affected by gradual but definite transformations. For example, in wealthier families, the wives supervised the domestic chores carried out by employed female staff and the children were educated by governesses.

The Role of Women Workers

In most European countries, women from poorer backgrounds worked from a very young age. Domestic labor, spinning, or the sale of products of craftsmanship were the most widespread tasks. In urban worker groups, it was common for wives to work with their husbands, although it was very rare for them to run a trade by themselves.

BUSINESSMAN
At this stage, the male head of the household became the main person responsible for income. Influential sectors arose from mercantile activities.

Childhood of the Poor

Among the majority of the population in Europe, childhood was tough and short. Children worked with their parents doing everyday activities. These were times of high mortality rates, and broken homes due to the death of both parents were common. In the early years of modernity, children were regularly orphaned or went to live with stepfathers or stepmothers.

RURAL WORK
In rural communities, the jobs of cattle tending, milking, and making cheese and butter were female activities. Until relatively recently, women were considered cheap, dispensable labor.

1 SUPPORTING EVERYONE
The head of the household was responsible for meeting the economic needs of all family members. He also provided for all the children and servants generally.

2 FAMILY LIFE
The wealthy urban population began to favor time spent with their closest family members. Leisure time was increasingly valued.

3 LADIES OF THE HOUSE
Many women became housewives, responsible for the full-time, nonremunerated work of looking after their husbands and supervising the bringing up and education of their children.

4 SHARED REARING
It was usual for women to give their young children to wet nurses, who breastfed them inside and outside the home. Wealthy families employed governesses.

Educating the Poor

Periods of starvation and plagues caused a crisis in the seventeenth century in Europe. These issues affected children in particular. Many communities collapsed and the numbers of orphans and abandoned children increased. A group of people, especially philanthropists and members of the various churches, began to tackle this situation and, in the search for solutions, gave education a central place. Standing out among them was the French Catholic priest Jean-Baptiste de La Salle (1651–1719), who was the founder of an innovative educational method.

Everyone to the Classroom

In 1679, La Salle founded a school for poor children in Reims, France. He later replicated the model in other city parishes and created the Congregation of the Brothers of the Christian Schools, considered the first institution for training teachers, to spread his pedagogical model. For the time, the innovations proposed were very original. First, a method was created for teaching in groups that left behind the old form of teaching one at a time. The pupils were grouped according to age in classes of thirty children, with long wooden benches and desks facing the front, where the teacher stood. The other major innovation was that the teaching was imparted in vernacular—French—and not in Latin, as it had been previously. This model spread rapidly, and La Salle decided to begin to train teachers using these guidelines. In 1706, he wrote a manual for their guidance called "La Conduite des Écoles Chrétiennes." He also developed education for work, institutes of correction for juvenile delinquents, rural education, and proposed a middle school that was more modern than the Jesuit College.

FACILITIES
The first schools were rooms annexed to the parishes.

Education for Girls

The Ursulines, the first congregation of nuns of Christianity, applied La Salle's model to the education of girls. Together with reading and writing, the girls were taught the supposed "knowledge of their gender," such as cleaning and embroidering.

SIGNUM FIDEI

CONGREGATION
"Sign of faith" is the motto of the current shield of the Christian Brothers.

① **TEACHER**
The teacher occupied the central position at the front of the classroom.

② **APPRENTICE**
Future teachers attended classes to learn the job of teaching.

③ **RELIGION**
Classrooms were decorated with religious items, such as crucifixes and images.

TIMETABLE
Lessons followed a standard timetable.

TECHNICAL SCHOOL
La Salle created schools for employment training.

LANGUAGE
The teaching was conducted in the vernacular.

RURAL TEACHERS
La Salle encouraged the training of rural teachers.

Lasallian Schools

One of the main characteristics of the Lasallian schools was that they were free of charge. The knowledge to be taught was limited to reading, writing, calculus, and the Catholic religion. There were numerous school rules and guidelines, and the teacher's role was central to the educational process. Classes were conducted in silence, which was maintained at all times. Pupils did not sit just anywhere; they were positioned in the classroom according to their performance and conduct.

BOOKS
Reading matter included catechisms and readings on religious themes.

PUPILS
They had to sit on benches in places previously assigned by the teacher.

VARIOUS TASKS
The pupils had the jobs of ringing the bell, distributing books, opening doors, and so on.

INSTRUCTIONS
The teacher controlled the pupils' individual work by means of questions and readings.

Discipline and Religion

I n 1534, Ignacio de Loyola founded the Company of Jesus, which rapidly became one of the key means by which to hold back the advance of the Protestant Reformation. Taking its organization from the military hierarchy, the Jesuit order depended directly on papal authority. They developed a series of activities to strengthen and spread the Catholic religion throughout the world, including by establishing missions in places as far off as China and the Americas. Education occupied a key place in them, from evangelization to the creation of universities, thereby establishing educational bases that would endure.

The Colleges

The main educational innovation of the Jesuits was the Colleges, created to train youngsters as officials of the absolutist states. In these, the education was based on discipline, expertise, and emulation. They were organized into camps of one hundred pupils under the leadership of a consul, and each camp was divided into *decurias* of ten pupils, led by a *decurio*. The *decurias* were recruited hierarchically. The first, called Rome, included the best pupils, and the last, called Carthage, included the weakest and least hardworking pupils. Just as each camp had another as its rival, so did each *decuria*. The individuals were paired up, and each soldier in a *decuria* had his rival in the corresponding *decuria*. School work involved continuous competition: the camp challenged the camp, the *decuria* struggled against the *decuria*, and the rivals watched over each other, mutually corrected and reprimanded each other.

La Flèche

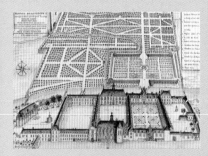

In 1603, Henry IV founded the renowned La Flèche Royal College in France, under the control of the Jesuits. It was subsequently converted into a military college.

Grand Hierarchy

The terms for organizing the classes made reference to the Roman army. The consuls commanded the *decurios*, and these their soldiers. Duties were assigned by professors depending on performance and obedience. The "table of honor" rewarded the best and stimulated competition.

1 MASTERS
The teachers were priests. They would explain their lessons and the pupils were expected to memorize and repeat their words.

2 DECURIAS
Groups of ten pupils headed by a *decurio* formed the basis of classroom organization and of the hierarchical system of education.

3 UNIFORMS
The attire combined military and religious styles, and symbolized the expected obedience and sobriety.

4 PUPILS
Pupils were never to be left to their own devices, so always had supervisors who accompanied them everywhere.

Presence in America

The Jesuits performed important educational work through a network of missions.

BOARDERS
In the colleges, there were annexed buildings in which some pupils lived. The rules were very strict, based on a military model.

RENÉ DESCARTES
Descartes was the most renowned pupil at La Flèche Jesuit College. He graduated in 1616 and then entered the University of Poitiers.

The Commercial Revolution

Under the new national monarchies, most notably those of Portugal, Spain, the Netherlands, and England, the Commercial Revolution marked a period of European economic expansion, colonialism, and mercantilism, and a fundamental change in the quantity

and scope of commerce. Commercial expansion was supported by technical improvements in seafaring, and from ca. 1450 explorations were made—first to Africa, then to Asia and the New World—by newly organized chartered companies. By 1700, the stage was set for the Industrial Revolution.

Men of Money

From the fifteenth century, the social position of European merchants improved considerably. The extraordinary development of long-distance trade between the East and the West meant an increase in the volume of items exchanged and also an increase in businessmen's earnings. Numerous dynasties or family companies of merchants were formed, with headquarters and branches spread throughout Europe. They gradually began to concern themselves with industrial and banking activities, lending money to political figures.

Economic Might

The commercial influence of Italian merchants became so important that at the beginning of the modern age they extended their operations throughout Western Europe. The high circles of political and ecclesiastical power depended on their merchandise and, above all, on loans from the major bankers for their personal or state projects. The lenders were renowned usurers, but it was very hard to avoid them when undertaking a major project. Numerous scholars have identified these commercial activities as the beginnings of capitalism. For example, the cloth merchants of the city of Florence bought wool abroad and had it worked by artisans in the domestic industry in exchange for payment of a few coins.

THE FLORIN—GOLD COIN
The growth of Florence prompted the issue of the florin, which was used for international transactions.

TRIBUTES
The merchants' wealth did not go unnoticed, and they paid tributes to the kings.

1

2

3

THE HISTORY OF COMMERCE

1460
STOCK MARKET
The first stock exchanges operated in the Netherlands and became economic centers of great influence.

NINETEENTH CENTURY
CENTRAL BANKS
The British government established the first national banking institution responsible for issuing paper money.

TWENTIETH CENTURY
GLOBALIZATION
The globalization of markets, the creation of international credit bodies, and the computerization of banking systems occurred.

The Italian Merchants

At the end of the Crusades, the major Genoese and Venetian merchants acquired a privileged position in terms of economic contacts between the East and the West. Urban growth and the volume of goods traded strengthened the influence of the bankers of these Central European port cities.

SPICES

Spices came from the Far East and were used to conserve and season food. They were also used as ingredients in medicines.

PORCELAIN

The best porcelain products came from China, where they were made with a mixture of local clays. They were both rare and expensive.

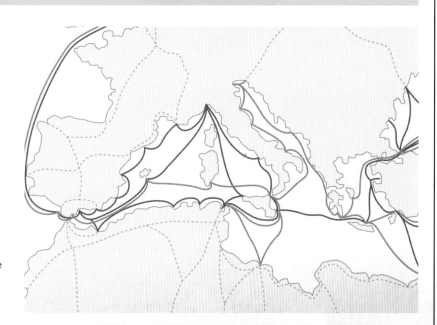

MARITIME ROUTES

Merchants crossed the Mediterranean Sea, arriving at the commercial centers located in the Black Sea and the regions controlled by the Hanseatic League in the North Sea.

MAP REFERENCES

Venetian routes
Genoese routes

1 MERCHANTS
The vast riches of the merchants enabled them to set themselves apart from feudal society.

2 EXCHANGE
Bankers issued letters of credit to trade between different currencies.

3 RETAILERS
Goods were sold in small quantities on the streets of the urban centers by retailers.

4 GONDOLIERS
Goods were transported between different sites by gondoliers.

PRODUCTS
Traded goods were announced in a loud voice.

SILKS
Luxury silks from the East were highly valued.

Trade around the World

They were personalities who transcended their time—all great merchants. But this was not because they laid the foundations for new ways of trading or for theories on commerce. Instead because their activities were the driving force behind the discovery of new regions, new cultures, and new ways of understanding the universe. Trade was the excuse that forced them to make contact with these other cultures, and thus extend their capacity and view of the world. Trade prompted Thales of Miletus to develop Greek philosophy and mathematics. Centuries later, Marco Polo arrived at the farthest edges of the known world through trade and presented it to Europeans in his classic book. It was the desire to trade with these remote areas that prompted Christopher Columbus, two hundred years later, to discover the presence of an entire continent on the other side of the Atlantic Ocean. And the marvelous adventures of Sinbad the Sailor showed the Muslim world view, customs, and depth of imagination to the rest of the world.

Thales of Miletus

GREECE
630-545 BC
The wisdom of Thales—a great mathematician and one of the fathers of Greek philosophy who studied the universe extensively—came into contact with different cultures through his work as a trader in his youth. However, his biographical details are somewhat sketchy and unreliable.

Marco Polo

VENICE
1254-1324
Born into a family of prosperous Venetian traders, Marco Polo spent seventeen years in the Far East, at the service of the Mongol emperor. On his return, imprisoned by the Genoese, he dictated his adventures to Rustichello da Pisa. The book *The Travels of Marco Polo*, opened a door to the Far East for Europe.

Sailors

With the exception of Marco Polo, in antiquity, the great journeys were only accomplished by sea. In addition to the dangers accompanying an overland journey, sailors experienced stormy weather, high winds, and waves, as well as navigational problems.

Christopher Columbus

GENOA
1436–1506

The discoverer of the Americas was motivated by trade. The idea was to open a trade route with the Far East, sailing westward to circumnavigate the globe, because the traditional land routes were blocked by the Ottomans and the sea routes by the Portuguese.

Sinbad the Sailor

ARABIA
EIGHTEENTH CENTURY

Sinbad is a fictional but very important character in the history of literature. The hero of a Middle Eastern cycle of folktales, he was added into European versions of *One Thousand and One Nights* when it was first translated in the eighteenth century. He is a Muslim trader who, after recovering his father's fortune, which he had squandered, goes to sea and experiences the most fantastic adventures.

"Travel eight days westward, you meet with cities and boroughs abounding in trade and industry, and quantities of beautiful trees, and gardens, and fine plains planted with mulberries, which are the trees on the leaves of which the silkworms do feed."

The Book of Ser Marco Polo, the Venetian
edited by Henry Yule

The Birth of the Bank

The concept of the bank is as old as the lending of goods by one person to another, in exchange for a small sum of interest. There are even references to very ancient institutions similar to banks in the time of Babylonia and ancient Egypt, thousands of years before the Christian age. Beyond this, with the appearance of money during the Middle Ages, and later, with the establishment of powerful commercial cities in northern Italy, the first banks began to operate.

Power and Risk

Starting from the fifteenth century, among its many innovations, the Renaissance brought about the dissemination of banking institutions—some truly powerful—which achieved a certain hegemony in Europe. The banks met the needs of merchants and the population in general, but they were also lenders to the great monarchies. Those first institutions received deposits, lent money, changed currencies, and issued and acknowledged letters of exchange to avoid the need for their holders to handle cash. These could be converted back into money, for example, in a faraway city.

The collecting of interest was a very complex point of conflict in the Christian world, because from the start of the fifteenth century, the Church prohibited usury. Nevertheless, this prohibition was gradually abolished. To be a banker in the early days of the Renaissance meant enormous power in most cases, although it always carried the latent risk of being expelled or imprisoned by the governors concerned (generally creditors). They were prone to level all kinds of accusations when they discovered that they were having difficulty in paying their debts.

Letters of Exchange

Letters of exchange, such as the one below, guaranteed conversion into money for their bearer, even in a different city from the one in which they had been issued. They could be endorsed and thus change hands.

Cosimo de' Medici, founder of the Medici Bank

THE MEDICI BANK
Among the numerous branches of this bank, the most curious was a traveling bank, which followed the pope's movements.

A contemporary calculation has it that the Medici family, during the fifteenth century, spent 18,000 florins of gold a year— a fortune.

The Medici were not just bankers. Their interests diversified into other businesses, such as major silk shops and wool factories.

Rise and Fall

The Medici Bank operated for a century, between 1397 and 1494.

It was in this bank that so-called "double-entry bookkeeping" was developed, which proved to be one of the most important contributions to the science of accounting.

On March 25, 1402, the bank opened its first branch in Venice. Later, it had many others in cities that include Rome, Geneva, Bruges, Lyon, and London.

A series of administrative errors, plus the inability to collect debts from major creditors, such as the British monarchy, and, finally, the invasion of Italy by Charles VIII of France, ended in the closure of the bank six years before the end of the fifteenth century.

One Day in the Bank of the Medicis

The Medicis were a powerful Florentine family. As well as providing politicians, members of royal families, and even three popes, they founded and owned one of the most famous and respected banking institutions in Europe: the Medici Bank.

The registers of the Medici Bank have been lost, but its history has been reconstructed to a large extent from the tax collectors' registers.

The Gold Florin of Florence

Among the many currencies that circulated in Europe, the most important was the Florentine gold florin, which dominated the market between the thirteenth and fifteenth centuries. It weighed 3.5 grams and was coined in almost 24-carat gold, the highest standard for the currencies of that age.

The First Bank

There is at least one bank that was founded in the days of the Renaissance that still survives today: the Banca Monte dei Paschi di Siena. Founded in 1472 by the magistrature of the city of Siena, in Italy, today it has 3,000 branches, 33,000 employees, and 4.5 million customers.

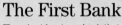
Like a modern bank, in the Medici Bank there were also cashiers, accountants, and managers.

The Art of Accumulating

A round the sixteenth century, Europe underwent profound social, economic, technological, and even religious changes. The old medieval ways of life—small, rigid, and closed— began to develop an unprecedented complexity. Suddenly, the world was made bigger by new discoveries; new industries flourished, as did new freedoms; and humankind's view of itself and its relationship with God and the state altered. In this context flourished the mercantilist idea that accumulation generates wealth, even if at the cost of others.

An Eye on the Balance of Trade

In the mercantilist view, the wealth of the world was set and constant, so what benefited some prejudiced others. Furthermore, wealth, which the powerful Church during the Middle Ages took a dim view of, was now regarded by states as a desirable goal, and was achieved starting with the accumulation of gold and silver. This could only be accomplished by increasing exports and restricting imports—that is, by achieving a positive balance of trade. This simple concept brought about endless complexities, for example, the need for the state (then predominantly absolutist) to participate to an enormous extent in the economy. Some countries, such as France and Great Britain, also understood the need to foster industry in order to generate exportable surpluses, and this, over time, turned them into economic powers.

NEW DISCOVERIES
The need to open up new markets and to be supplied with raw materials prompted expeditions and new discoveries.

Acquiring Gold

The accumulation of gold by the state was the ultimate goal for the mercantilists. It was achieved in three ways:

1 EXTRACTION IN THE COLONIES
This was the method chosen by Spain, which spent it to import manufactured goods.

2 WARS AND PIRACY
In the times of mercantilism, Great Britain developed the practice of sea piracy.

3 FOREIGN TRADE
It was necessary to export more than was imported. Hence the intervention of the state, which also encouraged industrialization, in countries such as Great Britain and France.

GREAT BRITAIN

Britain brought about strict controls, with the accent on international trade and less rigidity in the domestic economy. It fostered exports and restricted imports. It prohibited any foreign merchant from trading in England.

TRADE

Trade with England was monopolistic. The colonies could trade with only the Crown. The colonies sent raw materials and received manufactured products.

Protection and expansion

During the mercantilist centuries, raw materials flowed from the colonies to the Old World, at the same time as manufactured goods left for the colonies and other destinations. Many wars in this phase of history had their origins in zealous economic protectionism and the desire for expansion.

AFRICA

SPAIN

By not developing its industry, Spain had to import manufactured products, and therefore, make its protectionism more flexible. To this end, it spent the metal it obtained in the colonies. The result was a progressive impoverishment.

OCÉANO ATLÁNTICO

FRANCE

France began to boost its industry earlier than England, with protectionist measures and the promotion of exports. Characteristic products were those manufactured for royalty—luxury items for the monarchy and the upper classes, which had previously been imported.

WARS

The great powers attempted to expand their colonies and their monopoly markets at the same time as they protected their own.

Diagram of Mercantilism

During the mercantilist period, a positive balance of trade was the priority. For this, it was necessary to have a strong state exercising economic protectionism, supported by high customs duties, adequate laws, monopolies, colonialism, and, in some cases, an important industrial development.

IS PANIOLA

AMÉRICA DEL

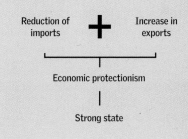

Winners and Losers

The diagram below shows the stages of European mercantilism.

1500	1600	1700	1800
Monopoly			
Spain powerful	Spain in decline		
	France powerful		
	England powerful		

Reduction of imports **+** Increase in exports

Economic protectionism

Strong state

The Slave Trade

During the sixteenth century, establishing European colonies in the Americas, and intensively exploiting the New World as a source of the raw materials coveted by Europe, demanded a huge quantity of labor at low cost. Mainly, there was a need for many people to work on the large sugar, cotton, coffee, and cacao plantations, the produce of which was sent to the Old World. Thus came about the slave trade, considered by some authors to be among the greatest tragedies of humankind, which in the sixteenth to the nineteenth centuries supplied the American colonies with African slave labor.

The First Great Global Tragedy

It is calculated that some twenty million Africans were enslaved and transported to the American colonies during the period—almost four centuries—that the slave trade lasted. The suffering of those who were captured, the subsequent sea voyage, and life in the Americas were unimaginably bad. Life expectancy was reduced to a minimum as soon as people were captured. In general, on the African continent, the capture and trading were handled by Africans and were closely linked with the wars between local ethnic groups. The human "merchandise" was delivered to the Europeans in the ports and crowded into slaving ships. The United States, although the largest colony, imported the fewest slaves. Brazil, on the other hand, imported ten times as many slaves and had the smallest colony, which indicates what subhuman conditions slaves were subjected to there. It was often more economical to make them work until they died of exhaustion and to buy new slaves than to keep them alive. From the eighteenth century, abolitionist movements would end this sinister practice.

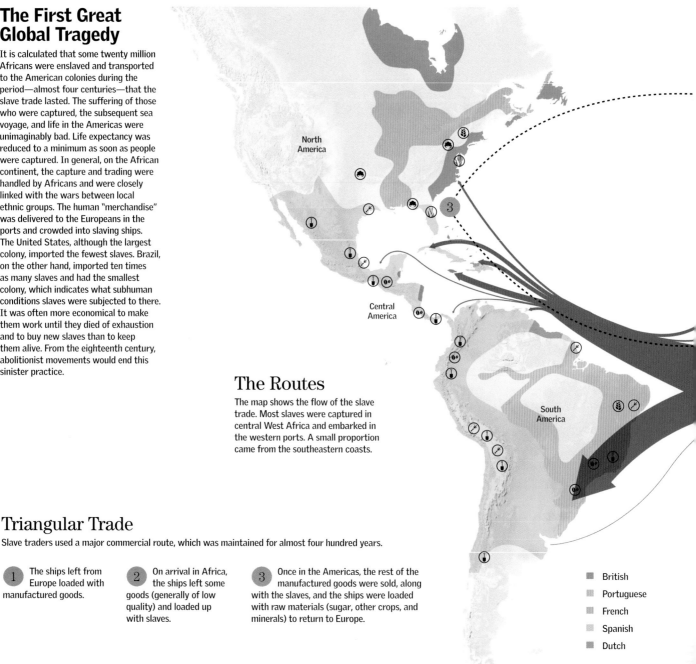

The Routes

The map shows the flow of the slave trade. Most slaves were captured in central West Africa and embarked in the western ports. A small proportion came from the southeastern coasts.

Triangular Trade

Slave traders used a major commercial route, which was maintained for almost four hundred years.

1 The ships left from Europe loaded with manufactured goods.

2 On arrival in Africa, the ships left some goods (generally of low quality) and loaded up with slaves.

3 Once in the Americas, the rest of the manufactured goods were sold, along with the slaves, and the ships were loaded with raw materials (sugar, other crops, and minerals) to return to Europe.

- British
- Portuguese
- French
- Spanish
- Dutch

The End

During the eighteenth century, the first abolitionist movements emerged, which bore fruit during the course of the nineteenth century, when slavery was abolished, putting a stop to the trade. The icon on the medal of the British Anti-Slavery Society, from 1795 (right), shows a slave imploring society: "Am I not a man and a brother?"

AM I NOT A MAN AND A BROTHER?

The Most Terrible Journey

Although it is hard to arrive at an exact figure, the most reliable estimates refer to a death rate of more than 20 percent during the crossing between Africa and the Americas. That is, out of every ten men who embarked, only eight arrived at the destination alive.

Asia

Europe

1

Africa

- ⊕ Mining
- ⊙ Coffee
- ⚘ Tobacco
- ✑ Sugar
- ⓦ Rice
- ⊛ Cotton

In the most inhumane conditions, every inch of the ship was used to house the slaves, who were shackled and unable to stand up or even to sit. The cargo was divided up into men, women, and children.

Understanding the Universe

In just 150 years, our conception of the universe changed drastically. In the early sixteenth century, Nicolaus Copernicus revolutionized astronomy and philosophical thought when he affirmed that the Earth is not in the center of the cosmos: it revolves around the Sun, and not the other way around, as the Church claimed. Despite proscription, astronomers, such as Tycho Brahe, Johannes Kepler, and Galileo Galilei, subsequently developed Copernicus' theory. Thus they took the first steps in what would become known as the Scientific Revolution.

A New Cosmos

In his book *De Revolutionibus Orbium Coelestium* (*On the Revolutions of Celestial Bodies*, 1543), Nicolaus Copernicus explained the movement of the planets. Until that time, the conception of the universe developed by the ancient Greeks still reigned supreme—particularly the theories of Ptolemy, who in the second century AD had postulated that the earth was a floating sphere around which the sun and the rest of the stars and planets revolved. Copernicus, who described anomalies in the Ptolemaic system, began to doubt his basic postulates and arrived mathematically at the conclusion that the earth moved, rotating on its own axis and around the sun. He revealed, at the same time, that the axis of the earth was inclined. His ideas gave rise to a new paradigm; they marked the beginning of the scientific revolution and laid the foundations for modern astronomy.

The Legacy of Copernicus

Many of his followers worked in royal courts, among these the Dane Tycho Brahe, the German Johannes Kepler, and the Italian Galileo Galilei.

HELIOCENTRISM

According to Copernicus, the sun is immobile and in the center of the cosmos; the planets revolve around it.

SPHE ASTR

Also k armill displa of the

Astronomical Evolution

In less than 500 years, humankind progressed from looking at the moon to stepping onto it. There are robot ships throughout the solar system, and telescopes in orbit have identified galaxies, black holes, asteroids, and even planets outside of our cosmic neighborhood.

NICOLAI CO PERNICI TORINENSIS DE REVOLUTIONIBUS orium cœlestium, Libri VI.

1543 COPERNICAN THEORY

Copernicus never considered publishing his work *On the Revolutions of Celestial Bodies* (left), but a disciple, Rheticus, persuaded him to do so and thereby changed history.

1610 *SIDEREUS NUNCIUS*

Galileo (left) published his first scientific treatise based on astronomical observations of the moon, the stars, and the moons of Jupiter using a telescope.

What Galileo Saw

The Florentine astronomer and physicist Galileo Galilei (1564–1642) was one of the most committed defenders of heliocentrism. He attempted to convince the ecclesiastical skeptics that there are mountains on the moon and that Jupiter has its own moons.

TELESCOPE
The instrument had been developed a year earlier, in Holland, but Galileo was the first to use it to look at the sky, in 1609. At that time, it was known as a "spyglass."

SCIENTIFIC METHOD
Galileo was one of the creators of modern scientific thought, combining inductive reasoning and mathematical deduction. His methods have been used since then in physics.

CONDEMNATION
The ecclesiastical hierarchy did not accept Galileo's ideas and condemned him for heresy in 1633.

SENATORS
Galileo gave the senators of Venice the rights to manufacture the telescope (although it was not his invention).

DOGE OF VENICE
In his first communication about his telescope to the doge, Galileo emphasized its military importance.

1755
GALAXIES

Immanuel Kant (left) postulated that the sun was one of the stars and certain nebulas were "island universes," today called galaxies.

1948
BIG BANG

The English astronomer Fred Hoyle used the term "big bang" for the first time to describe the explosion that gave rise to the universe, 14,000 million years ago.

1995
EXOPLANETS

The first extrasolar planet, 51 Pegasi b, was discovered. With instruments, such as the Hubble space telescope (left), several hundred more have since been detected.

Emerging Classes

T|he Industrial Revolution, which began in England in ca. 1760, provided the initial impetus for changes in social and economic interaction. As migrants arrived in the cities from rural areas to work in new factories, there was a rapid proliferation in the construction of cheap housing for

working people. Meanwhile, a powerful middle class, bolstered by economic success, established itself throughout Europe and the United States. A growth in the supply and standard of education was fed by a protectionist agenda that sought to maintain the national prosperity fostered by the new "captains of industry."

Under the Ground

From prehistoric times, human beings have obtained minerals and other materials from the Earth's crust. Miners' work is dangerous, and often gives rise to respiratory illnesses due to the inhalation of fumes and dust among other toxic materials. Today, the workers in the bowels of the Earth often choose this work because they belong to mining families and are proud of their job. They are recognized for their great spirit of solidarity.

A Dark Job

The main activity of miners consists in clearing the rock to extract minerals. However, they must also prop up the tunnels with wooden supports to prevent them from collapsing, open up paths for moving materials, and load the mineral onto trucks to be transported above ground. They spend many hours without seeing sunlight, only using the light from lamps, which today are attached to their helmets. The mineral permeates the workers' clothing and their whole bodies, with the work demanding considerable physical effort and carrying many risks to the individual. Respiratory illnesses—such as silicosis, which affects the lungs—are the most common conditions affecting miners.

Mine Shafts

Miners adopt forced postures or travel long distances stooping to reach the seam of the coal or material they are extracting.

WORK
Tools used include the pickax and shovel.

LOAD
The mineral is gathered together before bringing it to the surface.

Coal Mines

Great Britain's enormous reserves of coal explain the industrial potential developed from the eighteenth century. The accessibility of this resource combined with a vigorous iron and steel industry to provide cheap metals for the construction of machines, railroads, and basic infrastructures.

Collapses

Accidents due to rock falls were very common in the industrial age.

Child Labor

Children's small physiques were taken advantage of to gain access along narrow tunnels into the mines. They received lower pay than the adults.

Miners in History

Since the Paleolithic period, there is evidence of excavations of minerals used for various purposes. Nowadays, the deterioration of the environment due to strip mines provides one of the main objections to this type of activity.

4000 BC
Exploring the Ground

The natural caves (left) in Grimes, in England, are explored for the extraction of flint, a mineral used to make simple tools.

2600 BC
The Stones of the Empire

The Egyptians access the gold mines of Nubia to ensure the provision of this precious material honoring the pharaohs.

ON THE SURFACE
Wooden structures
were built to protect
the access points
and tunnels.

1 ADMINISTRATION
The offices of the
higher-ranking employees
were located here, from
where the instructions for
work were given.

2 TUNNELS
The construction of
tunnels, chimneys, corridors,
chambers, and ventilation
shafts was required.

ROPES
Minerals and tools were
raised and lowered via a
vertical shaft.

TRANSPORT
The mineral was
transported in trucks
on tracks.

LEVELS
Various wooden ladders
connected the tunnels
below the ground.

THIRD CENTURY BC
Hydraulic Mining

The Romans employ
water pressure to
detach rocky material
and remove sediment.
Engineers develop
techniques to fit the
circumstances.

TENTH CENTURY
Expansion of Iron

The armed conflicts that
characterize the centuries
of the Middle Ages
stimulate the exploitation of
this metal, which is used for
manufacturing all types of
weaponry and armor.

NINETEENTH CENTURY
Gold Fever

In 1848, thousands
of workers head to
California to look for
gold. Manual extraction
techniques are
combined with the
use of machines.

TWENTY-FIRST CENTURY
Deterioration of the Environment

Numerous mining activities
(left) have an impact
on the environment,
affecting biodiversity and
contaminating water sources.

Factory Days

The first industrial workers belonged to the British textile industry. They were craftsmen and farm workers, of urban or rural origin, who began to take on jobs outside their homes, together in the same location under the direct control of the boss of a workshop or his foremen. These bosses provided them with everything necessary to do the job—that is, they provided tools and raw materials. In exchange, the workers received meager wages that were barely sufficient to make a living.

Modern Times

Many people living in towns and cities in the eighteenth century had no property; they had no land or tools to satisfy their basic needs. For this reason, in order to subsist in the new industrial world, they had to sell their labor in exchange for a salary or cash wage. For the first generations of industrial workers, it was very traumatic getting accustomed to routines and strict discipline because these were totally unknown to them. The absence of labor laws meant that work systems were arbitrary and varied from factory to factory. Gradually, the workers joined together to demand better working conditions. Thus the first socialist and anarchist trade unions emerged, which held strikes and boycotts to claim wage increases, equal rights, and reductions in working hours.

Telegraphists

The development of communications was fundamental for the growth of trade. Telegraph lines even stretched across oceans.

SPACE
Because the machines were huge and costly, they could only be purchased by entrepreneurs and installed in factories.

DISCIPLINE
Foremen made checks on workers every hour to make sure they were being productive.

CLERKS
They were usually stationed in post offices.

CODE
The use of a code made up of a combination of dots and dashes allowed messages to be sent quickly over long distances.

Salaried Work

The strengthening of the capitalist system expands remunerated work and increases the workers' demands. The granting of rights to workers is slower than the technical innovations, the aims of which are to increase earnings and productivity.

1850
Child Labor

Since the Industrial Revolution, children are commonly present in the textile industry (left) due to their low cost and their small hands, which are ideal for operating the machines.

1900
Female Textile Workers

On March 8, 1908, female garment workers in New York march, demanding the vote, improvements in conditions, and an end to child labor. Two years later, International Women's Day is inaugurated to remember.

The Textile Industry in England

In the early stages of the Industrial Revolution, the cotton industry became the main activity. It incorporated various innovations into its weaving and spinning processes and displaced the wool industry in terms of its size.

1 STEAM
The major driving force behind technology was the steam engine, used as a source of energy in the iron and steel and textile industries.

2 LOOMS
The mechanical shuttle and spinning jenny were inventions that enabled finer, stronger thread to be made in less time.

3 COTTON
Coming from the British overseas colonies, cotton was a raw material that was cheap and easily supplied on the foreign market.

FACILITIES
The rooms were large but poorly lit.

PRODUCTIVITY
The steam engine allowed a reduction in costs and an increase in production.

INEQUALITY
Men and women worked equally but wages were unequal.

1920

Assembly Line

Taylorism and Fordism are established as systems of work. Time, coordination, and discipline are combined with the industrial assembly line, or chain (right).

1970

Workers Under Control

The emphasis on management and organization appear to be key in increasing Japanese productivity. "Toyotism" arouses admiration.

2000

Technology and Workers

Accelerated technological advances increase the need for specialization and concrete training for correct working performance.

City and Factories

I n the late eighteenth century, the process of industrialization led to migrations from the country to the big cities, where factories seeking employees were located and people could find work. Large numbers of cheap houses were built in the cities for the new working classes. Neighborhoods were formed with houses arranged in rows. There were few comforts and the homes were often located in unhealthy and unassuming settings.

Class Consciousness

Working-class areas were bustling and overpopulated. In them, people of all ages shared their routines and their misfortunes. It is estimated that the overcrowding here was one of the key factors in the creation of strong bonds of solidarity among workers.

1 **SHARED TOILETS**
Toilets were in a small room attached to the row houses. A number of families would use one; generally, a block of forty houses might have just six toilets.

2 **GROUND FLOOR**
There was usually a single room that was used as kitchen, living room, and dining room. Likewise, located in this space were austere items of furniture in which people kept the few belongings they had.

3 **SLEEPING**
Married couples and their children usually shared a single room upstairs that was used as the bedroom. Working-class families had many offspring, *proles* in Latin, which gave rise to the name "proletariat."

THE ATTIC
This was small and not all houses had one. It would sometimes be rented to unmarried workers.

WALLS AND ROOFS
The houses had thin, red brick walls, through which the noise from the adjacent houses could be heard. The roofs were made of black or blue slate.

ROW HOUSES
The arrangement of houses in rows allowed the maximum use of space. Sometimes there were as many as three rows of houses together. The first, with small yards at the back, were the most comfortable.

4 DOWN THERE
The basements were cheap-to-rent spaces that, generally, were very dark and damp. On occasions, they could be occupied by more than one family.

5 WASHING THE CLOTHES
Metal or wooden bowls were filled with water to wash the clothes. Generally, clothing was washed on the sidewalks and hung from the windows on lines.

6 DRINKING WATER
To start with, plumbing systems did not reach the working-class neighborhoods. Water was obtained from a shared pump.

Rural Houses

During the Industrial Revolution, the homes of country dwellers were also humble, although, in contrast with the urban homes, they did not experience overcrowding. They might have stables, areas for manual work, and barns. The families were equally large and shared all the daily tasks.

The Nuclear Family is Born

The Industrial Revolution, which began in England in the eighteenth century, brought about countless technological innovations in production, which gave rise to large-scale migrations from the rural sectors toward the big cities. In this context, families underwent hugely significant transformations: the bonds of kinship became looser and family relations were focused on a much smaller number of members. Thus the nuclear, or modern Western, family came about, made up solely of parents and their respective children. In the industrial process, a separation occurred between the home and the workplace, which in turn drew up the boundaries between the public and private space.

Change in Habits

The model of the nuclear family—that is, father, mother, and children—began to spread in the eighteenth century in the West. In cities, the recently arrived rural families had to adapt to new realities and customs that were unknown to them. The patterns of day and night for work and sleep no longer applied; instead, what marked the rhythm of work were clocks and clocking-in at factories. Furthermore, the form of subsistence changed radically: the family ceased to be the unit of production and was replaced by the individual work of each member. Since salaries were low and difficult to survive on, all the members of the family had to attempt to earn a wage. As the working environments were so wretched, the family became idealized as a perfect place of refuge compared to the urban working setting. Gradually, the distance between fathers and children was reduced and the social function of the woman as wife and mother was reevaluated. The liberal ideology born from the development of the middle class and of economic progress, for example, began to proclaim the individual's right to choose a spouse and a place of residence.

Living in the City

The change from rural to urban life was traumatic. Many women continued to wash clothes in the rivers near to the large cities.

CHILDHOOD POSTPONED

Industrialization began a process in which childhood was differentiated as a special stage of life. However, in the early days, children were exploited by the factory bosses or taken advantage of to perform jobs for which the pay was much lower than it was for adults.

OPERATING MACHINES

The introduction of various technologies into the field of work was the distinguishing feature of industrialization. Workers had to specialize in operating machines.

THE CHILDREN
The progressive incorporation of women into salaried work changed family life. On occasions, mothers left their children alone, so older children supervised the younger ones.

 THE FATHER
The man began to work outside of the home for a salary, and this became the family's main source of income.

 THE MOTHER
If she did not work, the mother's role was focused on providing emotional support and generally supervising the home.

 MOTHERHOOD
Having children meant the loss of employment for the mother. No special leave for motherhood existed.

MANAGING BY THEMSELVES
When both parents worked, the children helped with the chores at home. Many also worked in factories.

ALL THEY HAD
The belongings of the first working families were meager. They only had each other, their clothes, and items for cleaning.

UNPROTECTED
The absence of labor laws to protect employees made it easier to exploit those who were weaker.

Schools for Factories

During the eighteenth century, capitalism became established as a dominant mode of production. The Industrial Revolution, which began in England in around 1760, provided the initial impetus for the modification of previously existing forms of social and economic interaction. Factories, the proletarianization of the workforce, the growth of cities, new forms of energy, production in large quantities, the regulation of the working day, and the trade unionization of labor were distinguishing features of this period. It became necessary to train a new type of worker to impose control over children and to create new material, symbolic, and educational conditions for the population as a whole.

Discipline for the Masses

In 1798, Joseph Lancaster founded a school in England that hundreds of children could attend. It consisted of a single classroom, similar to a large shed, without any internal divisions, where a teacher taught up to 500 children at one time. It was based on a system of monitors—outstanding students who took the teacher's orders and passed them on to their classmates, who were grouped together in tens according to the subject being taught and regardless of age. The pupils were taught reading, writing, calculus, and religion. The classes were conducted in parallel; while one group learned writing on trays filled with sand, another did exercises from their benches, and a third learned reading by standing in front of a poster on the wall. This approach was similar to that used in the factories, with continuous movement and preestablished structures.

Learning How to Read

First the letters were taught, then syllables, and finally words and sentences.

ORDERS
"Hands still!"
"Clean your slate!"
"Write!"

Lancasterian Rigidity

Lancasterian schools operated using a system that combined rewards and punishments. The former ranged from giving toys and money to written congratulations and badges. The punishments, on the other hand, could be either physical, such as beatings, or symbolic, such as warnings, fines, and public humiliation. The aim was to maintain order by making the students fear such punishments.

1 MONITORS
Outstanding students who passed on knowledge to a certain group of classmates were called monitors.

2 STUDENTS
Each group of ten students received instruction on a certain subject. The groups were then rotated.

3 HIERARCHIES
The pupils' location in class indicated their position. The most outstanding sat near the monitor.

4 TEACHER
The teacher gave orders with shouts, claps, bells, and placards; the monitors interpreted these and passed them on.

PUNISHMENTS

DENIGRATION
Placards were placed on the children describing them in insulting terms.

PHYSICAL PAIN
Being forced to kneel on grains of rice.

BEATINGS
The teacher or monitor would cane the pupils.

HUMILIATION
Donkey ears, worn by those who made mistakes.

Teaching Method

Learning was mainly based on the students memorizing and repeating the information dictated by the teacher.

INSTRUCTIONS
The teacher addressed his students from a raised platform.

PREPARATION
Before the class, each monitor received the day's agenda.

Bathing

The contemporary idea of the bathroom includes contributions from various cultures and was developed over thousands of years. The Egyptians related bodily cleanliness to medicine and the Romans established the bathroom as an integral part of the private home. In the Middle Ages, these practices disappeared, with outside toilets being used for waste. From the nineteenth century, scientific and technical advances enabled complex bathrooms to be installed in family homes as well as the construction of sewer systems in large cities.

3000 BC TO 1500 BC
The Origins

The oldest drainage system, designed to remove human waste from homes, was built in Skara Brae, a Neolithic Scottish village. For their part, the Cretans designed washtubs and stone seats, which had cisterns supplied with flowing water.

300 BC TO AD 1500
From the Latrine to the Outside Toilet

The Roman Empire built public complexes of latrines in large cities that communicated directly with an innovative sewer system. In turn, rich Roman families spread the use of exclusive rooms with lavatories in their residences—their *domus*. In medieval times, the predominance of rural life meant that the toilet was moved outside the home. A few yards from the house there was an outside toilet with a deep well, which might possibly have had a comfortable seat.

1700 TO 1900
Modernity

The rapid changes that culminated in the modern bathroom occurred in Europe. Progressively, the bathtub and the bidet, which were usually located separately, were brought into the same room as the toilet, in a space dedicated exclusively to hygiene.

NEW FURNITURE
The search for greater comfort and distinction prompted the use of various furniture items and accessories.

 1 **THE ROMAN LATRINE**
The latrine in Roman times was connected to an urban drainage system. Sea sponges were often used for washing.

 2 **THE MEDIEVAL OUTSIDE TOILET**
The toilets of the medieval period had a wooden board with a hole in to sit on. The feces fell into the water of a well or into a receptacle.

The Bathroom

The bathroom of today came about from the association of ideas of well-being, health, and hygiene at the end of the nineteenth century. Also, the inclusion of paintings and carpets, among other things, indicated the aesthetic and functional importance of this space.

FALLING WATER
The therapeutic purposes of the shower were promoted in the late eighteenth century. It was eventually incorporated with the bathtub.

SOPHISTICATION
Contemporary architectural tendencies included windows and various accessories.

ORIGINAL GIFT
The first toilet with a water tank and seat was created by an English courtier as a gift for Queen Elizabeth I.

RAISED CISTERN
Operated by a hanging chain, the cistern caused a flush of water with considerable pressure.

RATED WASHSTAND
began washing their specially designed ith faucets.

THE FAMILY BATHTUB
In the nineteenth century, this started to be made in a specific shape to allow for bathing indoors.

Clean water

Drainage

Toilet

U-shaped bend

U BEND
This is a U-shaped pipe that allowed the expulsion of feces and prevented the entry of bad smells into the environment.

The Master Dresses Up

In the late nineteenth century, a powerful middle class had become established in the major European cities. Their houses, containing several floors, reflected their great economic success. The owners resided on the second floor, which was the most accessible, well lit, and ventilated part of the building. Its large apartments had luxurious, decorated rooms. More modest apartments on the third and fourth floors were rented by acquaintances. The basement and the attic—smaller, more uncomfortable spaces—were reserved for the servants or less wealthy people. In a certain sense, this unequal distribution of rooms in the middle-class house reflected the order and logic that governed the organization of capitalist society.

Buildings to Look At

The construction of dwellings with various floors was a symbol of the progress and rapid economic growth of the age. These buildings demonstrated the high social level achieved by certain middle-class sectors, and they aroused the envy of the urban dispossessed. The social and economic differences became increasingly evident in the crowded cities. Some wealthy families built sumptuous residences to relax in outside the cities.

Red House

The emblem of the emerging modern dwelling, "Red House" was the name given to the brick house built in the nineteenth century by English architect Philip Webb, commissioned by the artist William Morris.

1 MAIN DRAWING ROOM
This was where homeowners spent the most time. Particular attention was paid to its decoration in order to arouse the admiration of guests. Prominent on the walls were the portraits of the house owners, painted in oils and with imposing frames. Mirrors also featured, which gave a sense of space.

2 SPLENDID ENTRANCE HALL
The entrance hall was usually decorated with ornaments, carved furniture, small paintings, and had sculptures on show. Here, the main staircase also began, connecting all the floors of the house.

3 BATHROOM
To have a specific room for personal hygiene was a clear symbol of prestige and economic level. The toilet, mirrors, and bathtub were a luxury; it was not customary to have a bath every day.

4 WORK AND HOME
In the majority of these buildings, there were commercial premises on the first floor. These housed family businesses that could be accessed from the street.

FIRST FLOOR
The home was not here; the doors opened onto the sidewalk and did not allow privacy.

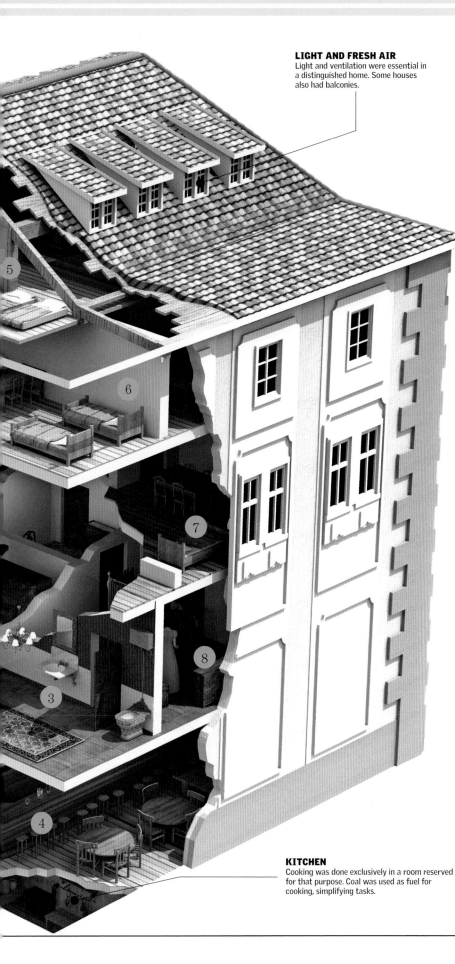

LIGHT AND FRESH AIR
Light and ventilation were essential in a distinguished home. Some houses also had balconies.

KITCHEN
Cooking was done exclusively in a room reserved for that purpose. Coal was used as fuel for cooking, simplifying tasks.

Looking Up

The middle class attempted to make sure that their neighborhoods reflected their situation of privilege with respect to the population as a whole. That is why they invested significant sums on top-quality materials and ornamentation.

5 ATTIC AND BASEMENT
It was in these spaces that the people who served the house lived. They housed generally small, poorly lit rooms, which would occasionally be rented out to poor people.

6 TO RENT
The third floor was usually rented out to middle-ranking families. Their homes were less ostentatious, but to share a building with a wealthy family offered prestige and other possibilities.

7 INTIMACY AT HOME
In this period, the curtains surrounding the beds of married couples for the purposes of privacy ceased to be used. The bedrooms themselves became intimate spaces.

8 SECOND FLOOR
This was the floor reserved for the building's owner and family. Its bedrooms were spacious and well laid out. Good lighting and easy access were its main advantages.

The Schoolmistress in Control

In the second half of the nineteenth century—with the consolidation of the nation states, the establishment of representative political systems, and the struggles of groups determined to spread literacy among the masses and extend the right to education—the elementary school became obligatory. To put the schools in place, it was necessary to implement a series of measures, such as the allocation of public funds, the construction of schools, the training of teachers, the diffusion of a universally applicable method, and the production of school equipment—from desks to textbooks.

Grades and Breaks

After the abandonment of the Lancasterian system (see pp. 196–197), in the nineteenth century a proposal was developed that would guarantee compulsory attendance at school. Known as the "traditional school," it was a reworking of La Salle's ideas (see pp. 168–169).

Its main tenets were the centrality of the teacher in the educational process, and an exclusive appeal to the pupil's intellectual functions, including reasoning and learning by rote. This is why it was necessary to maintain silence and keep the pupils still.

In turn, the pupils were organized into age groups, composed of no more than thirty members, called "years" or "grades." The alternating of instruction with intervals of rest and recreation; the combined teaching of reading and writing; an expansion of the subjects to be taught with civic training and notions of sciences, humanities, and arts; the prohibition of corporal punishment, and the evaluation of learning and the preparation of progress tables and reports by the teachers were just some of the innovations of the period.

Johann F. Herbart (1776–1841)

This German educator and philosopher developed a set of formal steps to be implemented in all classes based on psychology. He is considered the father of scientific education.

SCHOOL BOOKS
For the combined teaching of reading and writing, supported by illustrations.

IN FRONT OF THE CLASS
At her desk, the teacher corrected the pupils' work and prepared reports.

1

BLACKBOARDS
Because paper was expensive, blackboards were used for the initial teaching of writing.

Classroom Climate

A new type of classroom was created, based on healthy principles, such as ventilation, light, heating, and cleanliness. They had to have a rigid order: the pupils had to be lined up facing the front, from where the teacher dictated her lessons.

1 TEACHER
It was claimed that women were better teachers than men, especially in the early years of education.

2 PUPILS
In many countries, the laws favored the joint teaching of boys and girls, at least until the age of ten.

3 DIDACTIC MATERIALS
The walls were decorated with plates and posters on the topics to be taught, as a reinforcement strategy.

RAISING HANDS
Pupils had to raise their hand to ask to speak.

SCHOOL FURNITURE
The desks were designed according to the precepts of hygiene and order.

Training the Elite

The modern high school model was established in the nineteenth century. Its function was not to train the ordinary, but the outstanding, who would control the destiny of nations. It was not an obligatory stage for all, with the selection process reserved almost exclusively for white men, who sought to pick the "best" for the continuation of higher studies.

Modern High Schools

The new institutions had different names, depending on the country concerned, such as the *lycée* in France, *Gymnasium* in Germany, grammar school in Great Britain, and *instituto* in Spain. The majority had an approximate duration of between six and nine years, and children between the ages of ten and eighteen attended. Their curricula combined classical culture with modern languages, sciences, humanistic training, and sports. Their function was to prepare students for entry to university, so they had very little connection with elementary teaching. To finish school, very tough examinations had to be passed, some of which are still in existence. The teachers were university graduates, mostly from the middle class and aristocratic elites.

The Gymnasium in Prussia

These schools in Prussia became established in the educational reforms of W. von Humboldt in 1812. Their purpose was preparation for university.

LABORATORIES
The biological and natural sciences were taught using experiments with appropriate equipment and materials.

The School Environment
The high schools were generally located in imposing buildings in the cities or in mansions in the countryside for boarding pupils. They usually had splendid architecture, with classical and medieval references. They were divided up internally according to the various activities to be performed there, and were equipped with up-to-date, modern materials for conducting the lessons.

1

SOCIAL CLASS
Like their teachers, the vast majority of students came from the well-to-do and cultured sectors of society.

1 LABORATORY
In science classes, the teaching of theory was combined with practical work, teacher presentation and the conducting of experiments.

2 READING BOOKS
Pupils had access to well-equipped libraries to enable them to do their classwork. There was also reading material in the classrooms.

3 TEACHERS
Teachers had to be models of moral and intellectual conduct for their pupils as a form of identification of their social class.

4 UNIFORM
The students in some schools had to dress in a strictly formal manner to identify them as students of the school.

5 PRACTICE AND ERROR
There was work on laboratory equipment to conduct experiments, which sought to emulate the work of scientists.

6 BOYS
In the nineteenth century, only boys attended high school. Girls were gradually admitted into separate institutions.

TEACHER TRAINING
The teachers were university graduates, specializing in the teaching of a specific subject.

Evaluation
There was a system of tables and reports, where the grades obtained by the pupils in their work and examinations were shown.

SPORTS FIELD
There was a sports field beside or close to the school for physical education classes and practicing sports.

The Pinnacle of Achievement

The establishment of Europe's education systems was completed in the nineteenth century. The previous institutions, which bore very little relation to each other, were restructured into a cohesive whole that was unified in its guidelines and ordered hierarchically. The notional "levels of education" were constructed to give education a point of reference. This enabled the education system to be transformed into a broad form of social betterment and selection, which was of use to the expanding middle-class society. From then on, the aim was that it would no longer be due to origins or blood, but through their own merits, that each individual could achieve privileged places in the social structure.

Imperial University

The University of Paris might date back to the Middle Ages, but the Napoleonic Empire rescued it from centuries-long abandonment and transformed it into the pinnacle of the education system under a centralizing model. According to a decree from 1808, by Napoleon Bonaparte himself, all the schools and colleges of France were dependent upon it. This proposal's contents were modernized, a new internal organization was conceived, and various fields of knowledge were included. From then on, the teachers were mostly laymen and education came to depend exclusively on the central state, strongly limiting the power the Church had had over it until then.

FAÇADE
With a neo-Renaissance style, decorated with allegorical statues.

VICTOR HUGO
Writer, dramatist, and poet, 1802–85.

The Best Pupils

The University of Paris trained many of the most outstanding French philosophers, writers, and scientists.

HONORÉ DE BALZAC
Novelist, 1799–1850.

PIERRE CURIE
Physicist, 1859–1906.

MARIE CURIE
Chemist, 1867–1934.

The Sorbonne

The Sorbonne's current building was constructed between 1885 and 1901 on the same site as the original. It is composed of a series of buildings, which, as a whole, form an imposing edifice, in accordance with the image the institution wishes to project.

1 OBSERVATORY
This marked the entry of the sciences. It has a telescope open to the public.

2 COUR D'HONNEUR
A square central courtyard, used for academic meetings and events.

3 CHAPELLE
Built by Richelieu, the chapel stands out on account of its Baroque style and has a separate entrance from outside.

4 MAIN ENTRANCE
The entrance faces onto Rue des Écoles. The name refers to its medieval origins, where the schools stood.

A Symbol of Science

The height of the observatory marked the opposition between these new lay scientific buildings and the towers of the medieval churches.

ARCHITECTURAL STYLE
The architect Henri-Paul Nénot wanted to construct a science building guided by Haussmannian classicism.

THE GREAT MURAL PAINTING
Apollo and the Muses on Mount Parnassus by P. Dagnan-Bouveret (1852–1929).

Richelieu Amphitheater

The round amphitheater in the building is dedicated to the memory of the cardinal who revived the Sorbonne in the seventeenth century. Richelieu was buried in the chapel of the institution.

Modern Living

The world we live in today is the result of all of humankind's experiences throughout history that have led up to this point.

Buildings and structures, customs, and technologies may vary around the world, but the system of commercialism and capitalism forged by revolution and

evolution is almost universal. In today's world an individual's position in society is determined by their own potential and capabilities; our social structures are based on equality; our economies are based on complex technologies that are widely available to everyone; and rational thought governs our societies.

Desk Jobs

The word "office" derives from the Latin *officium*, meaning service or duty. Today, the office is a place for administrative work characterized by the presence of desks. Office workers are employees who work in a shared space, performing very diverse tasks. Employers have many ways of distributing the space in an office, depending on the activities of the company and number of employees. If the bosses prioritize communication and a sense of belonging to the company, they are likely to opt for shared spaces with few hierarchical differences. However, if they choose more private and silent areas for work, they may establish closed rooms or create cubicles.

For the Middle Classes

A growth in office work accompanied the development of the industrial world. Generally speaking, in the first factory establishments there were specific spaces for performing accounting and administrative tasks, and the offices were in the same building where production took place. Office workers were differentiated from the factory workers, earning better salaries, having better working conditions, higher levels of education, and forming the urban middle-class sectors of modern societies. As the years passed, these offices began to be separated from the centers of production and acquired specific organizational systems. In the early twentieth century, unified, shared spaces proliferated, reproducing the layout of school classrooms, to prevent employees from being distracted. Today, in contrast, many employers seek to prioritize comfort, teamwork, and communication among employees.

DISCRIMINATION

Married women with children had greater difficulties than single women in securing employment in the first part of the twentieth century.

SEDENTARINESS
Office workers are often sedentary.

MILESTONES OF OFFICE WORK

Advances in this field are closely related to the activities of the contemporary world. The speeding up of innovation occurred with industrialization, with the aim of arranging and optimizing the time that employees spent in the office.

900
THE SCRIPTORIUM

Monks working in the scriptoriums of monasteries (left) transcribe religious scripts and invent shorthand.

1868
TYPEWRITER

The first typewriter to meet with commercial success is invented by Christopher Sholes. The production of this technology is more or less standardized by the 1920s.

New Spaces

During the twentieth century, the enlargement of the tertiary (service) sector brought about an increase in the work carried out in offices. It became the norm for each worker to do their specific job at their own desk, on which were usually found a typewriter, paper, forms, and pens. As the century progressed, telephones and personal computers were gradually added.

BUREAUCRACY

An organizational structure characterized by explicit, regularized procedures, a division of responsibilities and specialization of work, a hierarchy and impersonal relationships. These are customary in office work places.

1 TYPEWRITER
Each of the keys was connected to a type, which had the corresponding characters or letters in relief at its other end.

2 PAPER
The paper was rolled on a cylinder on the typewriter. When reaching the end of the written line, a lever was used to rotate the cylinder.

3 TRAINING
Clerks studied typing to be able to type as quickly and as neatly as possible.

4 TOOLS
Working tools could include forms, pens, inks for the typewriter ribbon, and various rubber stamps.

5 CONCENTRATION
Office workers were usually supervised by high-ranking staff, who walked around at various times during the day.

FURNITURE
The desk is the essential item of furniture for office work.

1920
SWITCHBOARD

Work in offices changes with the introduction of telephones. Switchboards (left) make the work of receptionists and secretaries more efficient.

1950
BULK COPIES

Making copies of documents speeds up with the arrival of photocopiers. The use of carbon paper for handwritten copies is also useful.

1980
INFORMATION TECHNOLOGY

Computers revolutionize work in the office. They also alter physical organization; digital archives begin to replace paperwork.

Heights of Convenience

S tarting from the late nineteenth century, the landscape of the great cities of the world underwent a major transformation. At first, the development of the safety elevator and steel-framed structures allowed for the development of high residential constructions. Later, in the early decades of the twentieth century, the first skyscrapers appeared, housing offices and commercial activities. After the end of World War II, the need for a rapid reconstruction in Europe and the search for a hierarchical organization of urban space prompted the birth of new architectural practices. To this day, tower buildings offer convenience and various alternative forms of living space.

Conjunction of Factors

The combination of various factors, such as the industrial production of steel and the success of elevators, allowed for the proliferation of tall buildings.

1 RESISTANCE

Constructions containing a number of floors were possible due to the incorporation of two basic materials: concrete and steel. The combination of concrete reinforced with rods or plates of steel (reinforced concrete) permits structures that are resistant to the forces of compression, flexion, traction, torsion, and so on.

Steel girders

Concrete core

Hallway

2 UNSHAKABLE SUPPORT

With the introduction of steel structures, it became unnecessary, depending on the height of the building, to construct thicker walls.

Going Up

In the mid-nineteenth century, elevators for carrying people were invented. The system of cogs and pulleys gave them greater safety, and they soon became a fundamental factor in the proliferation of tall apartment buildings.

4 **EXTERNAL APPEARANCE**
The outer walls enclose the structure but provide no supporting function. For this reason, they may be made of various types of material, such as glass.

The Rationalist House

In the early twentieth century, the rationalist style in architecture spread throughout Europe. Among its key postulates: the dynamic conception of spaces, a predilection for simple geometrical forms, and the direct relationship between the form and function of spaces. The most well-known rationalist was French architect Le Corbusier (1887–1965).

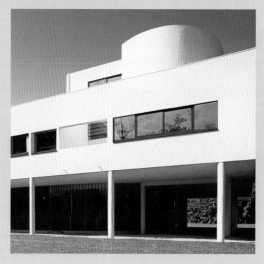

3 **STABLE BASES**
The first step in construction is laying the foundations—the part of the building that distributes the weight of the structure in the ground. The foundations may be deep or shallow, depending on the characteristics of the terrain and the size of the building to be constructed.

Building Materials

The earliest materials for construction were those that were found in the local environment. For example, Neolithic communities in the region of the Near East were pioneers in the use of adobe, working stone and incorporating bricks into the dwellings. Over time, these basic components were used by different cultures according to availability and their specific needs. In the nineteenth century, the rapid growth of industry on a worldwide scale diversified the materials used, speeded up the urbanization process, and triggered revolutionary architectural changes that have continued to the present day.

100,000–8000 BC
FIRST RESOURCES

Hunter-gatherer communities used the raw materials they found around them to build their temporary refuges.

6000 BC–AD 1700
URBAN CULTURES

From the first Mesopotamian urban communities to pre-industrial European cities, adobe, stone, brick, and wood were used for various purposes and in different procedures. In general, public buildings were constructed using more resistant materials, such as marble, whereas ordinary houses were built using simpler, less robust elements, such as mud or wood, among others.

1700–THE PRESENT DAY
THE INDUSTRIAL ERA

Reinforced concrete, steel, and glass were the construction materials used on a huge scale in the industrial era. For the first time, the distinctions between the materials used for major constructions and for ordinary housing disappeared.

WOOD
The quality of different types of wood meant it could be used in various ways in the Middle Ages.

STONE
In the Americas, the Incas were distinguished by their use of stones that joined together without cement.

ADOBE
In early antiquity, mud was mixed with straw and dried in the sun.

NATURAL ELEMENTS
In prehistoric times, shelters were made using branches, leaves, hides, and bones.

BRICK
Bricks in the ancient world were made of a clay agglomerate that was baked and then used to build walls.

Reinforced Concrete

In the industrial age, the use of concrete associated with an internal steel structure expanded. Reinforced concrete quickly became popular on account of its adaptability and its resistance to high temperatures. Its capacity to bear flexion stress meant it could be used in constructions of all types.

CONCRETE
Very resistant, concrete is produced using cement, sand, gravel, and water.

STEEL
Steel revolutionized construction with its qualities of both hardness and flexibility.

GLASS
Used in windows, glass is manufactured using a process called vertical drawing.

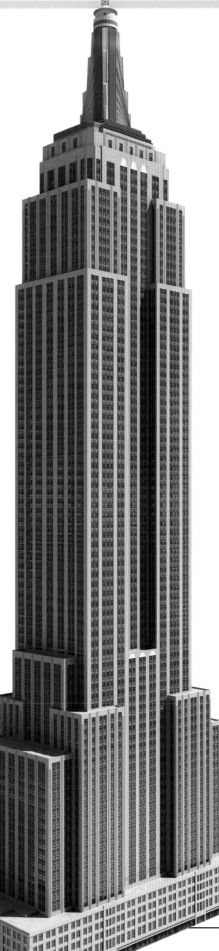

EMPIRE STATE BUILDING
Inaugurated in 1931, for four decades its 102 stories made it the tallest skyscraper in the world. Hundreds of reinforced concrete pillars bear its 365,000 tons.

Materials of the Future

The search for elements that suit the needs of both modernization and the environment characterizes the architecture of the twenty-first century. The new trends focus on the latest scientific advances, sustainable materials, and designs for constructions that respect nature.

NANOSTRUCTURES
These will be able to resolve specific issues in each project according to the molecular structure they possess.

COMPACT ELEMENTS
Quartz-silica agglomerates and glass can be employed in various colors and combine aesthetics and function in the same element.

COMPOSITES
In the future, composites of polymers combined with boron fibers or glass could replace reinforced concrete.

Links with the Future

Diversity is the common denominator in family structures around the world today. In some regions of Asia and Africa, the traditional systems of extended families, clans, or polygamy have persisted for centuries and have changed little. In the Western world, the nuclear family has gained prominence and, at the same time, new models of marriage and for bringing up children are more noticeable. The definitions of family, kinship, and marriage are becoming ever broader.

Imagining Families

Despite the marked differences on a worldwide scale, it is possible to outline certain tendencies in the Western world: the free choice of spouse, the extension of the rights of women and mothers, greater sexual freedom, and the inclusion of the rights of children and of those with disabilities in family and social environments. In recent decades, some issues that were hidden before, due to modesty or conservatism, began to be debated and analyzed in public arenas and also in private. Among these we could mention divorce, homosexuality, sexual satisfaction in marriage, the choice of marriage without children, cohabitation, and being single by free choice. Today, it is easier than before for children to live in a family with separated parents after a marriage breakup; relationships between people of the same sex are more accepted; and there is an increased tendency to evaluate whether or not to continue in a marriage on the basis of levels of personal satisfaction. These issues still reaffirm the predominance of the family as a basic, primary institution that unifies us as communities and as human beings. It is not disappearing, but it is constantly subject to transformation.

Proud to be Single

Men and women who remain single through choice are increasing in number in the more well-to-do sectors in the United States and Europe.

Same-Sex Unions

Many people have stable relationships with others of the same sex. In a growing number of countries, equal rights and the possibility of being fathers or mothers using assisted reproductive treatments are recognized.

EQUAL PARTNERSHIPS

Among the gay community, the legalization of gay marriage is an important concern.

New Forms of Association

In recent decades, and on a global scale, heterogeneous models and customs have arisen within families. These new core relationships face constant challenges to their internal structures, for example, those surrounding the upbringing of children and the application of parental control.

NUCLEAR FAMILY
This has been the predominant family model since the Industrial Revolution, despite the processes of modernization and constant cultural transformations.

Adult Children at Home

Economic difficulties or the comforts of home delay the flight of grown children from the family home. This tendency is evident in all social sectors.

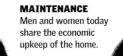

MAINTENANCE
Men and women today share the economic upkeep of the home.

COHABITATION
A term designating couples who are not married and who live together.

CHILDHOOD
It is considered special in law in modern societies.

DIVORCE
The breaking of the marital bond is usually accompanied by shared custody rights.

Eco-Houses

The industrialization and growing urbanization of most of the planet has had huge repercussions for the environment. Climate change and pollution have become some of the overriding global concerns. Architecture is now being used to contribute to the care of the environment. The so-called "passive house" focuses on taking advantage of climatic resources and saving energy; it maintains comfort levels inside using natural resources, such as sunlight, with minimal need for the use of conventional heating or cooling systems. It also involves the use of eco-sustainable materials.

Efficiency

A passive house is a construction that is very well insulated, practically sealed. In winter, the internal temperature is maintained through sunlight and the warmth produced by its occupants and electrical equipment inside. In summer, the orientation of the windows and protection against sunlight enable it to remain cool.

1 QUALITY MATERIALS
Appropriate materials are used, particularly wood made up of layers, which interlock so adhesives are not required. Once used, it can be returned to nature.

2 STORAGE OF RAINWATER
There are various systems for exploiting the natural supply of water. One of these is the installation of an underground tank that receives water from the roof's drainpipes and distributes it throughout the house.

SOLAR PANELS
Photovoltaic panels convert solar energy into electricity. They may be complemented by other systems.

SUSTAINABLE ARCHITECTURE
Starting with the use of natural resources and saving energy, the aim is for the house to have the lowest possible impact on the environment.

TEMPERATURE EXCHANGE
The used or stale air passes through a wheel or a structure of overlapping plates, with intermediate spaces, without mixing or having any contact with the pure air. However, its heat can be transmitted and used.

Stale air

Pure air

EXCHANGERS
These are panels that exploit the sun's energy to heat water. Hot water can also be used by the heating systems.

GREENHOUSE AND VEGETABLE GARDEN
This type of home usually has a space for growing food. Using a greenhouse allows diversified production throughout the year.

5 ## THE DRY TOILET
This consists of a toilet with two chambers to separate the excrement. It stores water, avoids the contamination of groundwater, and allows fertilizer to be obtained.

3 ## GLASS SURFACES
Large windows are orientated in the direction of the sun to allow the entry of light and heat. Hermetically sealed glazing reduces the loss of the heat received.

4 ## LOW-CONSUMPTION LIGHTBULBS
Compact fluorescent lightbulbs, better known as low-energy lightbulbs, require less energy than incandescent ones, and achieve the same level of illumination.

6 ## RECYCLED MATERIALS
There is a clear trend toward furniture made from recycled cardboard.

The Cyberhome

In recent decades, the intelligent or domotic house has been developed—that is, a new type of construction that incorporates a number of modern technologies within it. The operation of the equipment in the home is controlled and coordinated by IT programs, which, for example, close the window shades, water the yard, or turn on the central heating. It is possible to monitor these tasks from any computer with internet access.

The Brain of the House

Everything in the house is managed via a touch screen, which is generally located by the main door to the house. From there, all the movements inside the intelligent house are programmed and monitored.

INTELLIGENT
Although the orders are given by human beings assisted by sensors, the house seems to act and decide for itself.

DOMOTIC
The name "domotic" came about from the combination of two words: *domus*, the Latin for "home," with "robotics."

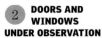
SECURITY CAMERAS
Cameras record what happens outside or inside the property. Actions can be controlled via computers, in the home, or remotely by cell phone.

DOORS AND WINDOWS UNDER OBSERVATION
Entry points are always monitored through devices, cameras, and sensors. The presence of intruders triggers lights to turn on and alarms to be activated. The whole process can be supervised remotely.

3 ECOLOGICAL LIGHTING
To save energy, the lights are turned off during daylight and turned on when there is less light due to rain or at nightfall.

DANGER
An alarm signal is activated if the start of a fire is detected.

THERE IS SOMEONE IN THE HOME
When there is no one inside the house, the security system simulates that someone is in. For example, the system can be programmed to close the curtains and turn on the lights at given times.

4 **ON SCREEN**
Everyday life and what happens in the rooms of the home appear on screens located inside.

5 **THE IDEAL CLIMATE**
Depending on the outdoor temperature, hot or cold air conditioning operates.

6 **YARD WORK**
The system for irrigating the yard is automatically activated, depending on the climatic conditions. The lawn mower operates in a programmed manner and charges its own battery when it is almost dead.

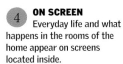

7 **THE BEST DIP**
Thanks to the controls installed in the swimming pool, the water temperature is always ideal. The same happens with the quantity of water; it is filled and emptied automatically.

8 **ATTENTIVE AWNINGS**
Depending on the climatic data received by the sensors, in the event of rain, for example, the awnings can open or close even when nobody is present.

Domobots

Mobile robots called domobots are connected to a domestic automation network. They are used in particular to perform tasks in the home, such as vacuum cleaning, washing, cleaning, or security.

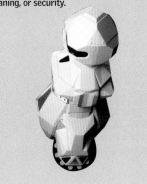

REMOTE SUPERVISION
Via the internet, the owners can control all activities, including turning the TV on and off when the children are alone in the house.

Under the Asphalt

When in December 1890 the City and South London Railway began to operate, Londoners saw the birth of a new era of urban transportation. The underground, or subway, which runs below ground, avoiding the thousand and one obstacles of large cities, especially the long traffic jams, is today an indispensable means of transportation for every major city on the planet. Millions of people around the globe move around using it every day of the week in approximately 160 cities.

Numerous Benefits

Subway systems around the world today have 5,000 miles (8,000 km) of rail track, served by 7,000 stations. Although the initial costs are very high, the benefits for cities are incalculable: the system allows people to be transported on a vast scale; it does not impose geographical barriers or restrictions, as happens on overground trains and on highways; it does not pollute; it does not worsen the noise levels of major cities; and, furthermore, it adds to the property values of the areas of the city it passes through. London has the most extensive network; New York the largest number of stations; and Tokyo and Moscow the highest number of passengers.

The Tram

A close relative of trains and grandfather of the bus, the tram had its glory days in the major cities between the early twentieth century and World War II. However, with their comfortable, silent new coaches and almost zero damage to the environment, several cities are now making trams part of their network once again.

A World Under the Streets

The expansion of the subway networks has generated a new type of space in the cities, where thousands of people, businesses, and trains coexist. The stations for transfer between lines are very complex, with their various levels and their numerous escalators.

Screens for information and entertainment.

Electrified third rail.

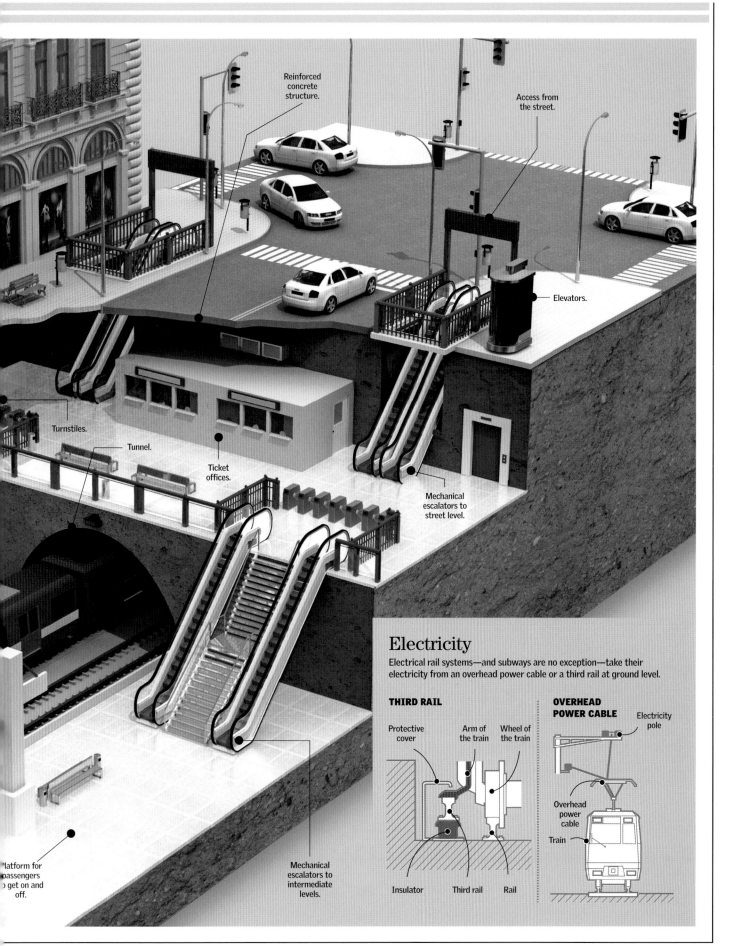

Reinforced concrete structure.

Access from the street.

Elevators.

Turnstiles.

Tunnel.

Ticket offices.

Mechanical escalators to street level.

Mechanical escalators to intermediate levels.

Platform for passengers to get on and off.

Electricity

Electrical rail systems—and subways are no exception—take their electricity from an overhead power cable or a third rail at ground level.

THIRD RAIL

Protective cover

Arm of the train

Wheel of the train

Insulator

Third rail

Rail

OVERHEAD POWER CABLE

Electricity pole

Overhead power cable

Train

Motherhood and Work

The inclusion of women in the labor market has brought about a transformation in family relationships, modifying the traditional role associated with homemaking responsibilities. Mothers have always worked and cared for their children and husbands, but they did so within the home. In the twentieth century, the rapid changes in the modern world meant that millions of women had to juggle their work outside the domestic environment with motherhood and marriage.

Multifunctional Woman

Women working outside the home led to changes within the family; it modified the role of fathers and reinforced the idea that during childhood people need special care. Although respect for gender equality inside and outside the home is not the same all over the world, conditions have improved in recent decades, but very slowly. In most cases, women who work outside their homes have seen their responsibilities increase, because their professional roles have been added to those they have as mothers and wives. That is, work outside the home has not displaced women's traditional roles inside the home, but added to them.

As a consequence, the sharing of domestic chores and childcare can still be an issue. For example, although some women may have a high status, society as a whole continues to regard them as responsible for maintaining an orderly home and bringing up the children. In this respect, it is very uncommon for a father who is head of the family not to go to work if one of his children is ill; it is "natural" for the mother to handle the traditional role inside the home. In the working environment, the key issues are disparity of earnings and the difficulty in gaining access to executive positions and breaking through the so-called "glass ceiling."

BREAST-FEEDING
It is recommended that babies are breast-fed for the first six months of their lives.

JUGGLING
Working mothers have to balance their work and home lives.

The Working Mother in the Twentieth Century

The inclusion of women in the labor market produced economic benefits, but it also created complications in terms of caring for the children and the home. The right to maternity leave was gradually extended.

WOMEN IN THE STRUGGLE
World Wars I and II increased the trend towards paid nondomestic female employment.

BIRTH CONTROL
The Pill allowed women, for the first time, to have in their own hands the possibility of planning their pregnancies.

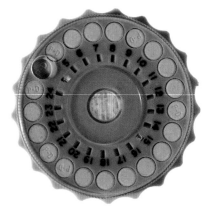

"TOGETHER—WE'LL WIN! OUR HEARTS ARE IN OUR JOBS!"

Large Steps

The fact that there are increased numbers of women in the workplace has been attributed to a combination of factors, according to the social stratum and the country concerned—for example, female self-determination, economic needs, and their role as the main breadwinner, among others.

COMPATIBILITY
The world of work, as an integral part of society, seeks to structure itself in such a way that women can live a satisfactory personal and family life.

1

BETWEEN TWO
Work is more satisfying when women share childcare responsibilities at home.

Legislation by Gender

In parallel with efforts to assimilate women into the world of paid work, on an equal footing with men, there has been progress in laws protecting and distinguishing the rights of women workers in the areas of maternity leave and special leave.

2

1 **HOME OFFICE**
New technologies enable many women to keep connected to their work from home.

2 **LEAVE**
In many countries, maternity leave is now commonplace.

3 **IN THEIR OWN RIGHT**
Women sometimes take advantage of motherhood to embark upon independent work projects.

3

The Twentieth Century and Beyond

One of the most salient features of the current era is that everything and everyone is increasingly connected to everything and everyone else, due to the exponential growth, commercial centrality, and infrastructure of the internet affecting every aspect of our lives. Ideas about progress going forward into the twenty-first century revolve around interpreting and improving the means of networked connectivity, incorporating the societal values that have evolved over time, and continuing to communicate the importance of our "human capital." Space exploration also looks set to grow in the future.

A Virtual and Digital Classroom

I n recent years, education has undergone a revolution that has led to revised approaches and new solutions. The appearance of digital forms of communication and information presents a series of new possibilities. Hyperconnectivity, the almost immediate access to various types of information, the large-scale distribution of laptops for pupils and teachers, and necessary technological adaptation are just some of these changes.

Learning from a screen

Around the mid-twentieth century, texts were generally presented in classrooms in two different ways: by voice—of pupils and teachers, and by writing—on paper or the blackboard. Since then, and with ever-increasing influence, a new medium has burst onto the scene: the screen. From the early slides and television sets to the current netbooks and notebooks, new possibilities, advantages, problems, and risks associated with their arrival have hit the classroom. Digital classrooms have sought to integrate the contributions of the old forms of teaching with the new. Added to the use of books, explanatory lessons, group work, and research are the use of educational software programs, higher output from pupils, and the implementation of multimedia resources.

PRINT

LAPTOP COMPUTER

Remote Education

Pupils can now have their lessons away from the classroom. Generally, this type of digital education is organized around moderators: teachers who regulate the content and level of discussions, organize the materials virtually and conduct appraisals. The moderator does his work without the need for direct contact with the pupils.

CONNECTIVITY AND DIDACTIC RESOURCES

Deliveries by e-mail

Digital library

Exercises with audio and voice

Circulation of information

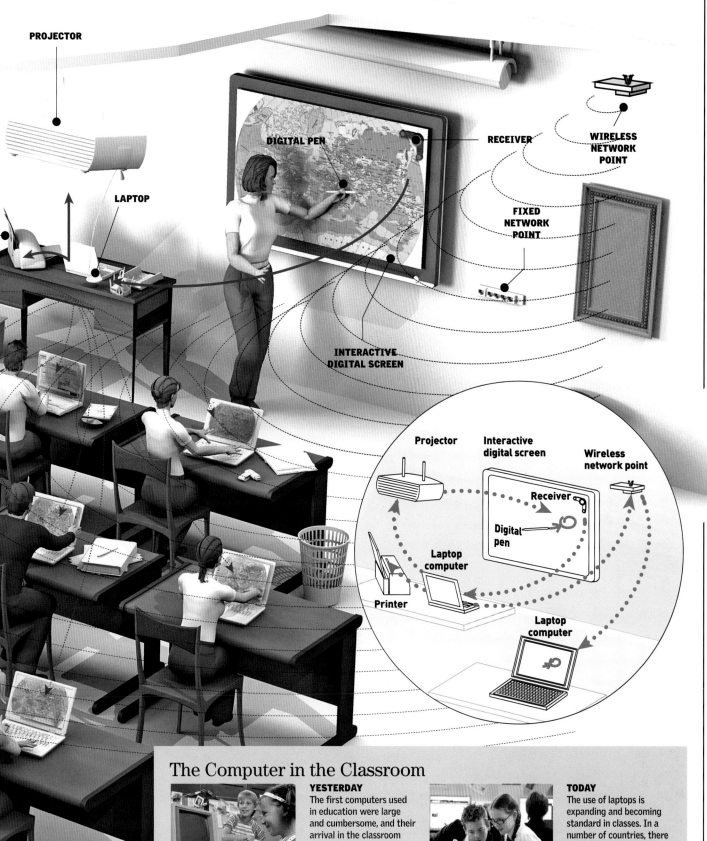

PROJECTOR

LAPTOP

DIGITAL PEN

RECEIVER

WIRELESS NETWORK POINT

FIXED NETWORK POINT

INTERACTIVE DIGITAL SCREEN

Projector

Interactive digital screen

Wireless network point

Receiver

Digital pen

Laptop computer

Printer

Laptop computer

The Computer in the Classroom

YESTERDAY
The first computers used in education were large and cumbersome, and their arrival in the classroom marked an extraordinary event. Pioneering schools added them in the 1980s.

TODAY
The use of laptops is expanding and becoming standard in classes. In a number of countries, there are state programs for their free distribution in classrooms.

From the *Gynaeceum* to Equality

In the past, a monopoly on knowledge and education was one of the main ways of exercising power. By these means, some people reserved access to certain information for themselves and denied it to the public at large. One of the groups most affected by this phenomenon was women, who were excluded from certain educational practices. However, there were movements that sought to change this situation.

Struggles for Equality

Classical culture sought to limit the actions of women to the domestic space, the so-called *gynaeceum*—specific rooms within the home environment to which they were limited. As it happened, some women were able to break this restriction. Outstanding among these was the philosopher Hypatia of Alexandria in the fifth century. In the Middle Ages, women had very limited access to certain fields of knowledge. One of the few opportunities to gain access to education was in convents, where nuns learned to read and write. Subsequently, the women of the aristocracy were able to be educated in court, and the first literacy projects on a large scale appeared. With the success of the school system of the twentieth century, women began to be educated en masse. Furthermore, they gained a profession that until then had been reserved exclusively for men: in teaching. Throughout the world the feminization of the profession took place.

Beyond these advances, access to medium and higher levels of education continued to be denied to women. Even if the regulations did not bar them, university was monopolized by men. In the twentieth century, a number of pioneering women broke through this barrier.

DIFFERENTIATION
In ancient times, it was claimed that men and women had nothing in common and their education should be distinct.

PRIVATE LESSONS
Individual education for the girls of the wealthier classes.

ANCIENT GREECE
The gynaeceum was the space reserved in the houses of ancient Greece for the exclusive use of women, segregated from the area inhabited by men.
It was located far from the entrance, on the upper floor or at the back of the building, to keep the activities and movement of women under control.

CONVENTS
From the Middle Ages, some women opted for the convent as a way to gain access to the knowledge that was forbidden to them, as in the case of Sor Juana Inés de la Cruz in colonial Mexico.

THE GOVERNESS IN THE NINETEENTH CENTURY
Based on the model of the classical educator and the Renaissance tutor, the governess taught the families of the upper classes at home. She taught good manners and religion, as well as reading and writing.

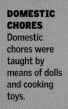

DOMESTIC CHORES
Domestic chores were taught by means of dolls and cooking toys.

JUST FOR THE FEW
Even if, exceptionally, some women began to gain access to education, for the vast majority the home environment continued to hold sway.

CONQUESTS
The struggle for equality in education was linked to the battle for votes for women.

Women at University

The few women who had the possibility of gaining access to university in the nineteenth century did so as "exceptional cases," and they tended to study medicine. Over the course of the twentieth century, the large-scale entry of women into all careers gradually took place.

NO DISCRIMINATION
Today, equality of opportunity is sanctioned by international agreements.

FUTURE HOUSEWIVES
For a long time, in the schools exclusively for women, the so-called subjects "of their gender" were taught, aiming to prepare wives and housewives who did not need to be interested in social life. The subjects included home economics, embroidery and darning, cooking, cleaning, and childcare.

MIXED CLASSROOMS—TWENTIETH CENTURY
The proposals for coeducation—the teaching of boys and girls together—date back to the late nineteenth century. The first cases had certain restrictions, such as the age of the pupils or the need for these lessons to be given by women teachers. The method was extended and consolidated in the twentieth century, and is still applied today in the twenty-first century.

Learning and Enjoying

In the early decades of the twentieth century, educators and teachers planned to transform education by introducing new methods, updating educational content, and relaxing the way in which institutions were run. They aimed at an education that promoted peace and freedom. The spread of such education was stimulated by the powerful impact that the horrors of World War I had on the conscience of humanity in the 1920s.

Sharing Everything

In various parts of the world, in the early twentieth century, alternative and experimental approaches began to be employed. Celestine Freinet in France, Ovide Decroly in Belgium, Maria Montessori in Italy, and John Dewey in the United States, among others, prompted innovations in the schools they managed. This diversity of practices led to the New School being considered more as a set of experiences than a single proposal. In them, it is possible to identify two elements that contrasted strongly with the traditional school: first, putting forward the pupil as central to the teaching process; and second, activism—bringing out the educational possibilities of "doing." The institutionalization of the New School occurred at the end of the second decade of the twentieth century in the United States, with the creation of the Progressive Education Association, and in Europe in 1922, with the International League for New Education, or the League for New Education, which organized a series of congresses in the 1920s and 1930s.

CHANGES FOR ENJOYMENT
The building was modified to allow for various activities, particularly expressive ones.

NO UNIFORM
In contrast with most English schools, at Summerhill there is no uniform.

ALEXANDER NEILL (1883–1973)
A Scottish educator who, not happy with the traditional school, founded his own school, Summerhill. He tells of the experience in his various writings.

Summerhill, for a Different Kind of Teaching

The motto of Summerhill school, founded in England by Neill in 1921, is "education for freedom." Despite several attempts to close it at various times, it is still running and maintains its fundamental philosophies.

FREE CHOICE OF SUBJECTS
The pupils decide when to study and which subjects.

THE IMPORTANCE OF PLAY
The dimension of play is part of the basic education.

ART AND THE EXPRESSIVENESS OF THE BODY
It is vital to stimulate creativity and imagination.

EQUALITY
The treatment between pupils and teachers is egalitarian.

TODAY
Today, the school is run by Zoë Neill Readhead, the founder's daughter.

GROUP DECISIONS
Discipline is decided by the pupils and implemented during assemblies, which take place every Friday afternoon.

OPEN AIR
The school is located in a remote place in the countryside to allow closeness with nature.

From the Floor to the PC Table

The history of education and schools is also the story of the objects necessary to put teaching into practice. Among these is the furniture, especially the place where pupils must sit to learn. The history of the desk enables us to understand the various material, technological, theoretical, and practical issues that over the centuries have influenced the way we learn.

Taking a Seat

In the first civilizations, the pupils would usually sit on the floor, in positions that recalled religious postures. Later, with the consolidation of reading and writing, new furniture, such as desks with lecterns, appeared.

When mass education became widespread in later centuries, it became necessary to seat as many pupils as possible.

Around the nineteenth century, the desk became the subject of major debates in which teachers and educators, doctors, and architects participated. Treatises were written on the subject and international conferences were held to discuss their variations. What ended up as the successful model was a hard desk bolted to the floor, which on the one hand prevented the pupil from being distracted and on the other prevented the development of illnesses caused by poor posture.

In the twentieth century, the New School proposed building desks that suited the size of the child, which could also be moved to perform group work. Today, the need to accommodate computers and new technologies has again stimulated the debate over possible new designs.

POSTURE
The back and legs are positioned according to the location of the board.

DESIGN
Stone and wood lecterns to support the weight.

EGYPT, ON THE FLOOR
Egyptian scribes learned a way of sitting on the floor and maintaining a straight back, a posture that facilitated concentration on the task at hand.

MIDDLE AGES, WITH BENCH AND LECTERN
Desks and lecterns enabled the handling of the large, heavy books they worked with.

MODERNITY AND THE SHARED DESK
The need to reduce costs meant that children sat on long benches and at shared tables during the nineteenth century.

Material Changes

The materials with which school desks were made followed general technological changes of history. In the nineteenth century, they were made of wood and metal, and in the twentieth century various types of plastic were incorporated. This allowed the development of an important industry that employed many workers, generating patents and conflicts between manufacturers. Furthermore, important architects and engineers worked to create useful modern designs, following education- and health-related prescriptions.

JUST WOOD
A single piece: seat and desk.

WOOD AND METAL
A desk with space inside, in which to keep useful items.

PLASTIC ARRIVES
A plastic seat and removable wooden tray.

The Low Tables of Buddhist Classrooms

The way of sitting is very important and is regulated in Buddhist temples. The tables are low and arranged facing the altar. The pupils sit on the floor behind them. The objects they use, from their clothes to the furniture, have certain colors that they identify with the tasks to be performed. Their bodily position allows them to concentrate better for meditation, reading, and writing.

FURNITURE FOR INFANTS
Seats and desks are adapted to the size of the smallest pupils.

COMPUTERS
Their use requires access to electricity and a connection to the internet.

NINETEENTH CENTURY: INDIVIDUAL DESK
In order that teachers could identify each pupil and have stricter control over their discipline and behavior in the classroom, the pedagogy of the nineteenth century introduced individual desks into schools.

TODAY, TABLE FOR COMPUTERS
The design of desks today incorporates the need for a more flexible classroom and that of being able to use IT and digital objects.

A Logistical Challenge

Generally, goods do not just go from port to port or from railroad station to railroad station. Usually, a number of different forms of transportation are used. From the point of departure, a commodity may travel by train, boat, and plane before it reaches its destination. This requirement has challenged the ingenuity of those who specialize in logistics to devise the shortest possible journey, at the lowest cost, while generating the least risk for the merchandise. Multimodal transportation is common in countries with more developed economies and is delayed to varying degrees in developing countries.

Multimodal and Intermodal

If a commodity's journey involves at least two different means of transportation, then it involves multimodal transport. However, to avoid risks in the handling of the merchandise, and to save on the time between loading and unloading operations and the economic cost that that brings, the concept of intermodal transportation has been developed. For this, the goods remain intact, in the same receptacle, from the point of departure to the point of arrival. In this type of transportation, it is the container that is most important. A commodity is housed inside a container. This, in turn, is loaded onto ships, trucks, freight trains, and even airplanes. In some cases, a truck loaded with a container can even be loaded onto a freight train or into a ship's hold. In any event, the aim is always that transportation by truck, which is the most costly and least efficient method, covers the shortest possible distances. The longer distances are covered by trains and ships.

A Little History

Although multimodal, and especially intermodal, transportation boomed in the 1950s as a result of the emergence of containers, the concept began to be used much earlier in the early nineteenth century.

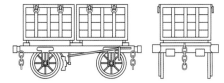

Containers for coal belonging to the Liverpool & Manchester Railway (Great Britain) from 1830.

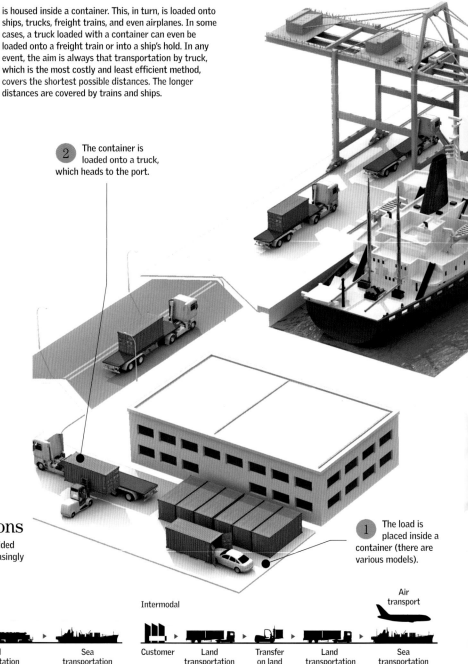

2 The container is loaded onto a truck, which heads to the port.

1 The load is placed inside a container (there are various models).

One-Thousand-and-One Options

The diagram below shows just some of the possibilities provided by intermodal transportation. The movement of goods increasingly requires true specialists in logistics.

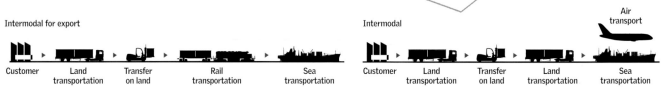

Intermodal for export

| Customer | Land transportation | Transfer on land | Rail transportation | Sea transportation |

Intermodal

Air transport

| Customer | Land transportation | Transfer on land | Land transportation | Sea transportation |

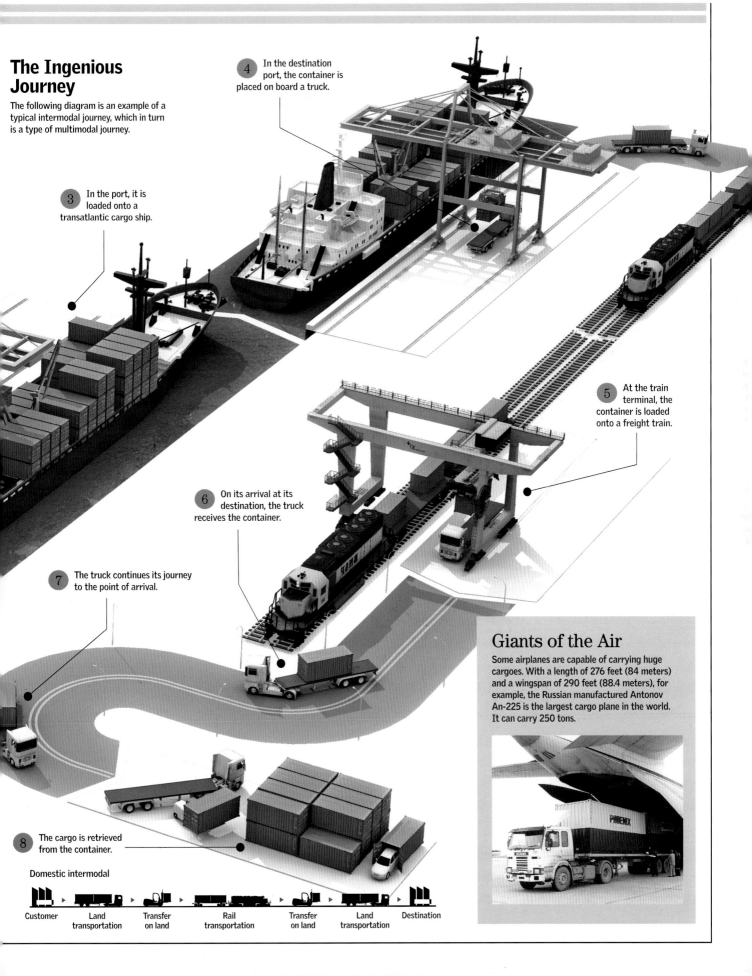

The Ingenious Journey

The following diagram is an example of a typical intermodal journey, which in turn is a type of multimodal journey.

3 In the port, it is loaded onto a transatlantic cargo ship.

4 In the destination port, the container is placed on board a truck.

5 At the train terminal, the container is loaded onto a freight train.

6 On its arrival at its destination, the truck receives the container.

7 The truck continues its journey to the point of arrival.

8 The cargo is retrieved from the container.

Domestic intermodal

| Customer | Land transportation | Transfer on land | Rail transportation | Transfer on land | Land transportation | Destination |

Giants of the Air

Some airplanes are capable of carrying huge cargoes. With a length of 276 feet (84 meters) and a wingspan of 290 feet (88.4 meters), for example, the Russian manufactured Antonov An-225 is the largest cargo plane in the world. It can carry 250 tons.

Thanks to the Sea

Humankind has fished since prehistoric times as a complement to hunter-gatherer activities on land. However, it was not until the twentieth century that exploitation of the sea on a large scale and international commercialization began. The development of refrigeration chambers, vessels with internal combustion engines, and industrial plants in ports enabled transoceanic fishing to begin and revolutionized the development of the fishing industry. At the present time, overfishing and illegal fishing are serious threats to marine biodiversity and require systematic and effective supervision by the watchdog organizations.

Finding Schools

Over the course of the twentieth century, fishing boats increased their cargo capacities, incorporated mechanized methods for handling nets, introduced scientific and technical advances to improve the detection of schools, and, above all, allowed the cold storage and transportation of fish over large distances. Fishing fleets have sonar systems that locate and establish the size of schools of fish and determine the species to which they belong. Some ships possess huge trawling nets that go to depths of up to 1 mile (1.5 kilometers), while others use mesh nets that are very effective because they allow the fish's head to pass through yet catch the gills, although these are only used up to 100 feet (30 meters) below the surface. The fishing industry is presenting numerous challenges at the present time. One of them is the limited diversity of consumer demand. Of the 22,000 fish varieties that are suitable for consumption, just six account for half of all catches: herring, cod, tuna, mackerel, anchovy, and sardine. The main producers and consumers of the fishing industry are the most developed countries. In the last decade, China, for example, increased its consumption by 35 percent.

CLASSIFICATION
After landing, cleaning and grading are carried out.

Fishing Boats

Industrial vessels have decks, closed areas, and refrigeration chambers for processing; small fishing boats come in various types, do not have decks, and can be driven by sails or oars.

FACTORY SHIPS
These are based in the most developed countries.

FILLETING
Once filleted, the fish are placed in cold storage chambers.

DEEP-SEA FISHING
The largest ships locate the schools using sonar waves.

From the Fishing Port

The concentration of services in ports is a central characteristic of the evolution of the fishing industry. This allows various essential processes to be performed faster and more cheaply, such as docking, the handling of fish, and the supply of the equipment necessary for fishing.

1 LANDING
Fish are brought to land in baskets or plastic receptacles containing plenty of ice to conserve it and delay the onset of bad odors.

2 DISTRIBUTION
The type of truck used for distribution depends on the size of the catch. For example, fish meal does not require closed refrigeration chambers.

TRANSPORTATION
They must have sealed boxes to prevent the leakage of liquids.

HYGIENE
The surface of the cargo compartment must not be absorbent.

REFRIGERATION CHAMBER
The air is cooled by liquids or gases. Today, a large proportion of the produce tends to be frozen.

READY TO DELIVER
The pieces of fish are distributed according to previously placed orders.

PRODUCTS FOR SALE
Whole, filleted, and packed or canned, a large variety of types of fish and seafood are offered at fish markets and in the supermarket aisles.

OVERFISHING
Illegal fishing and overfishing attack ecosystems, damage small-scale fishermen's livelihoods, and impoverish the natural food supplies of marine mammals.

Bulk Commodities

In the modern world, there are types of goods traded in large quantities, the quality of which practically does not vary, even if they are produced in different countries. They are the so-called commodities. In general, they are raw materials, such as farming products and minerals, for example, without the addition of industrial processes, and they are usually traded in bulk. Commodities are usually very important for the economies of developing countries, which have a low level of industrialization, and their value is one of the most important indicators of the world economy.

From Oil to Bank Notes

It is possible to divide commodities roughly into two groups. On one hand there is fuel, such as oil, coal, and natural gas. Then nonfuel commodities, including foodstuffs (cereals, sugar, wheat, and corn), beverages (coffee, tea, and cocoa), metals (copper, aluminum, and zinc), and agricultural raw materials, such as wool and cotton, and much more besides. In some cases, financial assets, such as money, are considered commodities, although as such they have special characteristics. The value of these products is uniform throughout the world and they are traded on special markets. Commodities can also be traded on futures markets, which favor speculation. The financial crisis that erupted in 2008 caused huge fluctuations in the value of commodities, which today struggle to recover their value.

Standard Quality

There are dozens of commodities and, in general, they are characterized by being raw materials or products with a very low level of processing and with a standard quality.

Winners and Losers

When the prices of commodities rise, it favors the emerging economies, while the industrialized countries that demand them, and the major consumers of food, see their trade balances suffer.

Fluctuations

During the first decade of the twenty-first century, the processes of development in countries such as China and India produced a great demand for commodities, which led to a rise in prices. Investors then discovered an attractive field for speculating and earning money, which led to even greater increases. However, the eruption of the world crisis in 2008 slowed down demand and discouraged investors, which caused a considerable drop in prices. Today, albeit with fluctuations, commodities are attempting to recover.

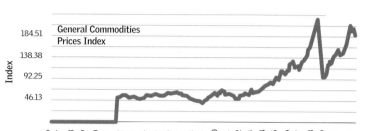

General Commodities Prices Index

Index

184.51

138.38

92.25

46.13

1986 1987 1988 1989 1990 1991 1992 1993 1994 1995 1996 1997 1998 1999 2000 2001 2002 2003 2004 2005 2006 2007 2008 2009 2010 2011

Futures Markets

Commodities are bought and sold on the world markets. But these transactions can be performed in advance, giving them the price that, in theory, the commodity will have on the day when the transaction will be executed. This speculative practice, which moves millions, also influences the prices of products.

From the Market to the Shopping Mall

Starting from the nineteenth century, a new way of offering products to the public was to completely change their shopping habits, first in the West and later at a global level. That was when the first department store opened: an enormous store on various floors, divided into departments, where the public could find products of all types at more affordable prices, and take advantage of special offers. Buying in the department stores was not only a new and attractive experience, but also a symbol of status.

New Vendors; New Buyers

The new commercial models that have flourished for approximately the last century and a half have involved new ways of buying and selling, and also of doing business. The large department stores, a special type of store where every brand has its space, began to coexist with shopping malls. Some department stores specialized in specific products, such as clothing or tools. Alongside the old street market, where food was bought, the major supermarkets emerged, and some businesses began to form chains—that is, to open up branches in other areas of the city, other regions of the country, or even abroad. The head office and its branches might belong to the same owner or else operate through a system of franchises, where one person participates in the other's business. The panorama is completed with globalization and the appearance of the internet, and with it e-commerce.

ADVERTISING

The brands present their products via various forms of advertising, giving rise to an industry that moves billions of dollars a year throughout the world, and tests the imagination of advertising creatives.

THE SUPERMARKET
This way of shopping, where the buyer serves himself with the products he wants to take away and settles the bill at a fixed point, arose in the United States in 1916 and rapidly spread throughout the world.

DEPARTMENT STORES
These arose in France in 1852. They consist of large buildings, of various stories, divided into sections. The whole business belongs to the same company.

Taste Lies in Variety

Never before have buyers had so much variety in terms of what is offered, nor have vendors had so many possibilities of offering their products. Commerce also reveals traces of its evolution in its variety.

COMMERCE AT A DISTANCE

This boomed at the end of the nineteenth century. Orders and deliveries were made by mail. Starting with the development of the worldwide web, consumers could buy products with a computer and an internet connection without leaving their homes.

THE SHOPPING MALL

This is an indoor space of large dimensions, shared by a number of various brands. They usually have spaces for leisure and relaxation as well as food services. They probably arose in the Middle East centuries ago, in the indoor sections of traditional markets.

THE REGULAR STORE

These boomed in the Middle Ages and haven't changed much to this day. The buyer enters the space of the seller, who then serves the buyer.

Sales

Sales and special offers are a very important part of today's commerce. Products lowered in price, free delivery, two-for-one offers—these are all used to tempt possible buyers and convince them that, if they do not buy, they are missing a unique opportunity.

THE STREET MARKET

This is probably as old as civilization itelf. Stall holders conglomerate at a specific point in the city (a square or a street), and offer their own products (whether prepared themselves or bought from others) directly to buyers.

FRANCHISES

These are stores that share a business model under the same brand. The owner of the site pays a franchise fee to the owner of the brand and undertakes to respect certain aesthetic choices and, generally, to provide a certain type of product.

Infinite Market

There are no borders. The internet has changed everything. Today, there are no limitations of supply and demand. The offer made, via the internet, reaches customers all over the world. And for those customers, the offer can also be global. In addition, e-commerce is changing our preconceptions regarding product advertising and is accelerating the business of goods transportation. Another challenge that is fast developing is that of forms of payment, with electronic money, and increasingly complicated security requirements to avoid scams.

An Old Story

The huge boom signified by the appearance of the internet and, almost immediately, e-commerce, may make us forget its origins—that the concept of remote trade already existed decades ago. What has changed, more than anything, is the dynamics, starting with the development of that powerful tool that is the internet, in a context of increasing globalization at all levels. Already in the nineteenth century, there were antecedents of trade via the mail service, money orders, and cash on delivery. During the 1980s, in the United States, a form of commerce called "direct sales" was prevalent; products were offered on television with full-blown audiovisual catalogs, and sales could be made over the telephone or even sealed with money transfers by credit card. This system—which still exists and is very popular—has given way to trading over the internet since the 1990s, when, in addition to the online divisions of known brands, major virtual department stores such as the now famous Amazon made their entry.

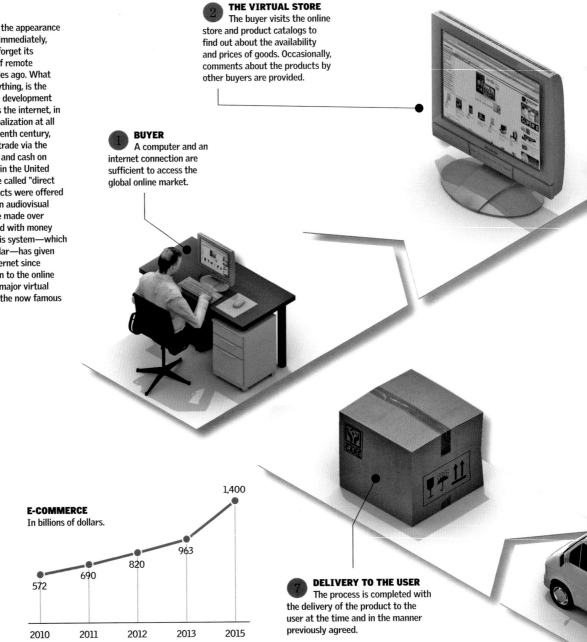

2 THE VIRTUAL STORE
The buyer visits the online store and product catalogs to find out about the availability and prices of goods. Occasionally, comments about the products by other buyers are provided.

1 BUYER
A computer and an internet connection are sufficient to access the global online market.

7 DELIVERY TO THE USER
The process is completed with the delivery of the product to the user at the time and in the manner previously agreed.

Limitless Growth?

The rate of growth of e-commerce is significant. It is estimated that in just three years, turnover for online sales will be nearly double that of today.

E-COMMERCE
In billions of dollars.

Year	Value
2010	572
2011	690
2012	820
2013	963
2015	1,400

The E-Commerce Circuit

From the online purchaser to the delivery of the product, a complex but fast path.

3 THE VIRTUAL SHOPPING CART
The buyer loads the products of interest in a virtual shopping cart or trolley.

Buyers per Region

With the exception of Africa and the Middle East, around the globe more than 80 percent of internet users have already made purchases online, which gives an idea both of the current power of e-commerce and of its potential.

4 PAYMENT
This can be made with electronic money or in cash on delivery of the product.

Credit
Debit
e-wallet

What do people buy on the net?

Almost half of the people who purchase online buy books. Approximately one-third buy clothes and airline tickets, while one in four people buy electronic goods and make hotel reservations.

Books 44%
Clothing 36%
Airline tickets 32%
Electronic goods 27%
Hotels 26%

5 WAREHOUSES
The warehouse receives the purchase order and the address to which the product must be sent.

6 TRANSPORTATION
The goods are sent to the buyer.

Electronic Money

All money transfers used by the telecommunications network, especially the internet, are called electronic money. There are various systems (credit or debit cards, bank transfers, and so on), although one of the latest innovations is payment by cell phone.

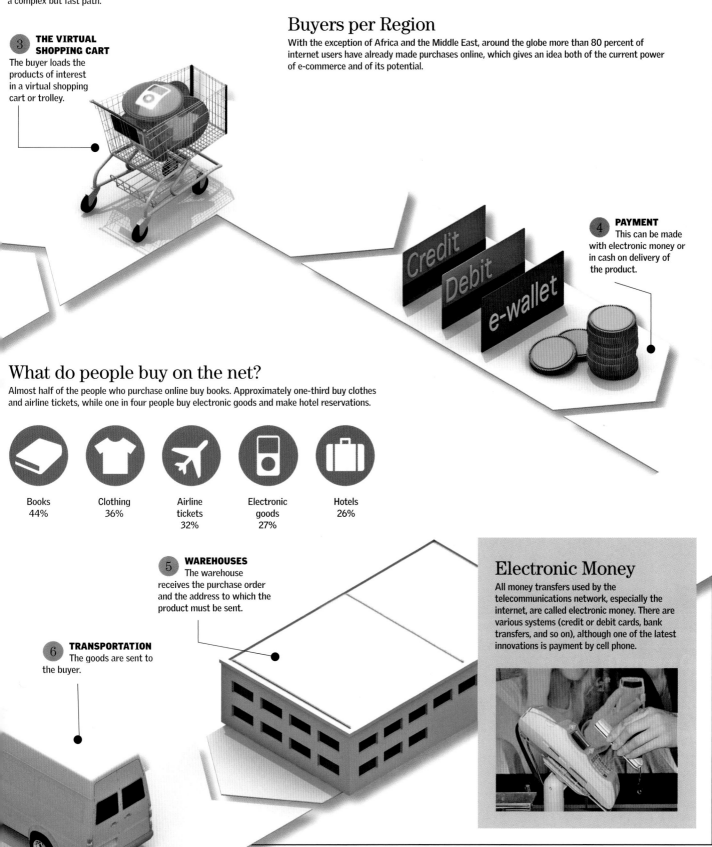

Virtual and Digital

S ince the late twentieth century, the speed of technological transformation has created new professions and changed the working environment. Huge numbers of workers offer their particular services without leaving their homes, and major companies have established commercial relations on a worldwide scale through virtual internet connections. These new forms of work present major challenges, such as the coordination of activities and the fast flow of communications. Key variables, such as better quality of life, work flexibility, productivity, and minimization of costs are now important considerations for both individuals and employers.

Challenges at Work

Work strategies and company structures are constantly changing, following the development of new technologies. In this context, virtual and digital working methods arouse controversy. For some, these systems tend to achieve higher productivity, lower administrative costs for companies, and a better work–life balance for employees. For others, these tendencies only contribute to reducing companies' responsibilities toward employees, thanks to the lower, or zero, employer contributions they generate. In any event, the companies using these structures are on the increase. For example, at IBM, 42 percent of its employees work from home or outside the office. The methodology of the eight-hour day in the office, working under constant supervision, is now much questioned. Many companies have been able to minimize their administrative costs. The article "How to ... manage the 'virtual worker' phenomenon" (2007) shows that IBM has managed to save a hundred million dollars a year on real-estate costs.

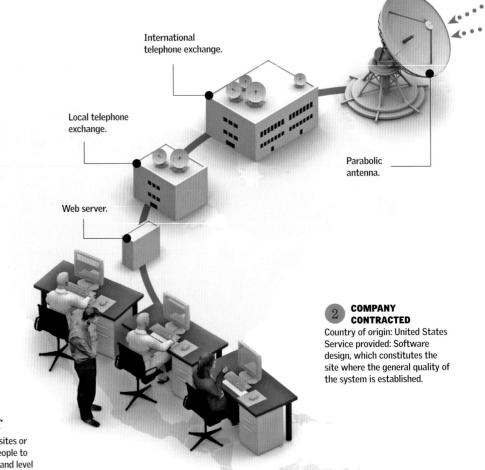

International telephone exchange.

Local telephone exchange.

Web server.

Parabolic antenna.

2 COMPANY CONTRACTED
Country of origin: United States
Service provided: Software design, which constitutes the site where the general quality of the system is established.

Moderator
Companies with websites or forums can recruit people to regulate the content and level of comments or discussions.

TECHNOLOGY IN EVERYTHING

The majority of modern professions are complemented with skills in information technology. However, some jobs depend entirely on these new technologies.

GENETICIST

This is a person who is skilled in diagnosing, preventing, and treating congenital defects attributable to any cause, both at an individual level and in the population at large.

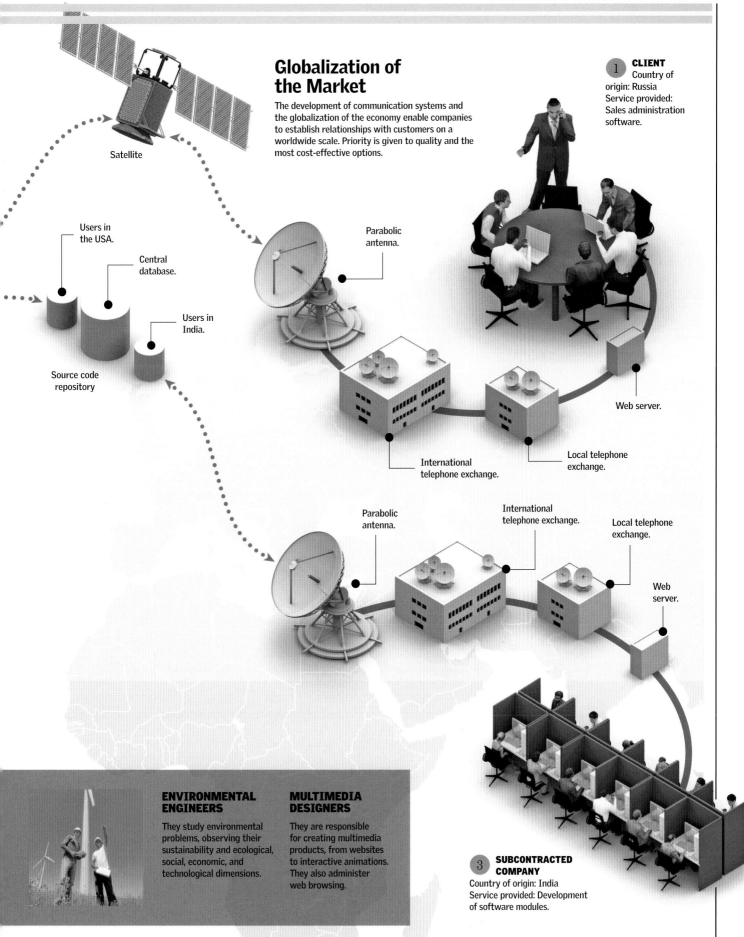

Globalization of the Market

The development of communication systems and the globalization of the economy enable companies to establish relationships with customers on a worldwide scale. Priority is given to quality and the most cost-effective options.

Satellite

Users in the USA.

Central database.

Users in India.

Source code repository

Parabolic antenna.

1 CLIENT
Country of origin: Russia
Service provided: Sales administration software.

Web server.

International telephone exchange.

Local telephone exchange.

Parabolic antenna.

International telephone exchange.

Local telephone exchange.

Web server.

ENVIRONMENTAL ENGINEERS

They study environmental problems, observing their sustainability and ecological, social, economic, and technological dimensions.

MULTIMEDIA DESIGNERS

They are responsible for creating multimedia products, from websites to interactive animations. They also administer web browsing.

3 SUBCONTRACTED COMPANY
Country of origin: India
Service provided: Development of software modules.

Space Challenge

Even today, many years after the epic lunar journey, it verges on the incredible to think of manned trips into space. The complications and costs are so high that ever since the day when the first man left the planet, in 1961, voyages into space have been limited; the roundtrip service between Earth and the International Space Station, at an altitude of about 250 miles (400 kilometers), is the closest thing we have to a regular transportation system through space.

The Time of Tourism

For now, the great innovation of the twenty-first century is not new spaceships capable of reaching the stars, nor even manned flights to other planets. In actual fact, it is the beginning of the age of space tourism. Until recently, everything concerning the transportation of people in space had been dealt with at government level by a handful of countries: the United States, Russia, and, most recently, China. However, it seems likely that in the coming years private efforts will be focused on taking people beyond the atmosphere for tourism and leisure. Even so, the imagined days of space bases spread out across the solar system, and even the galaxy, with regular passenger services, still seem to be a distant goal.

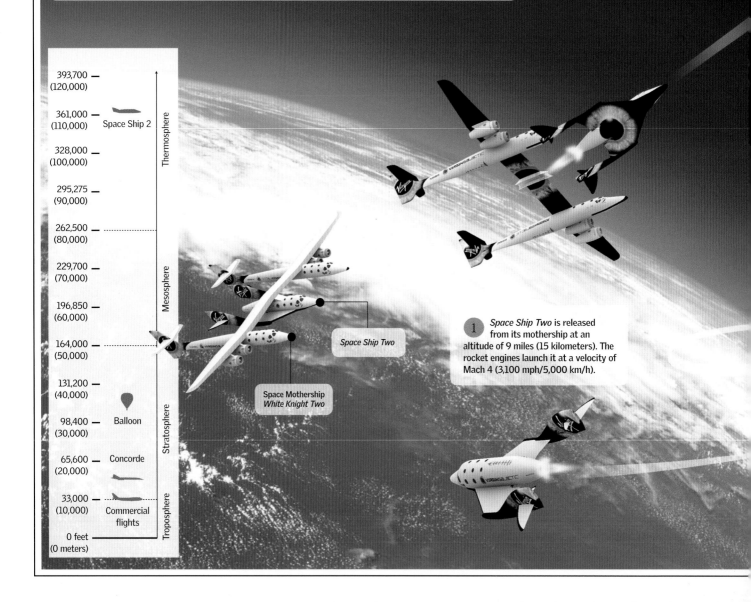

393,700 (120,000)

361,000 (110,000) Space Ship 2

328,000 (100,000)

295,275 (90,000)

262,500 (80,000)

229,700 (70,000)

196,850 (60,000)

164,000 (50,000)

131,200 (40,000)

98,400 (30,000) Balloon

65,600 (20,000) Concorde

33,000 (10,000) Commercial flights

0 feet (0 meters)

Thermosphere

Mesosphere

Stratosphere

Troposphere

Space Ship Two

Space Mothership *White Knight Two*

1 *Space Ship Two* is released from its mothership at an altitude of 9 miles (15 kilometers). The rocket engines launch it at a velocity of Mach 4 (3,100 mph/5,000 km/h).

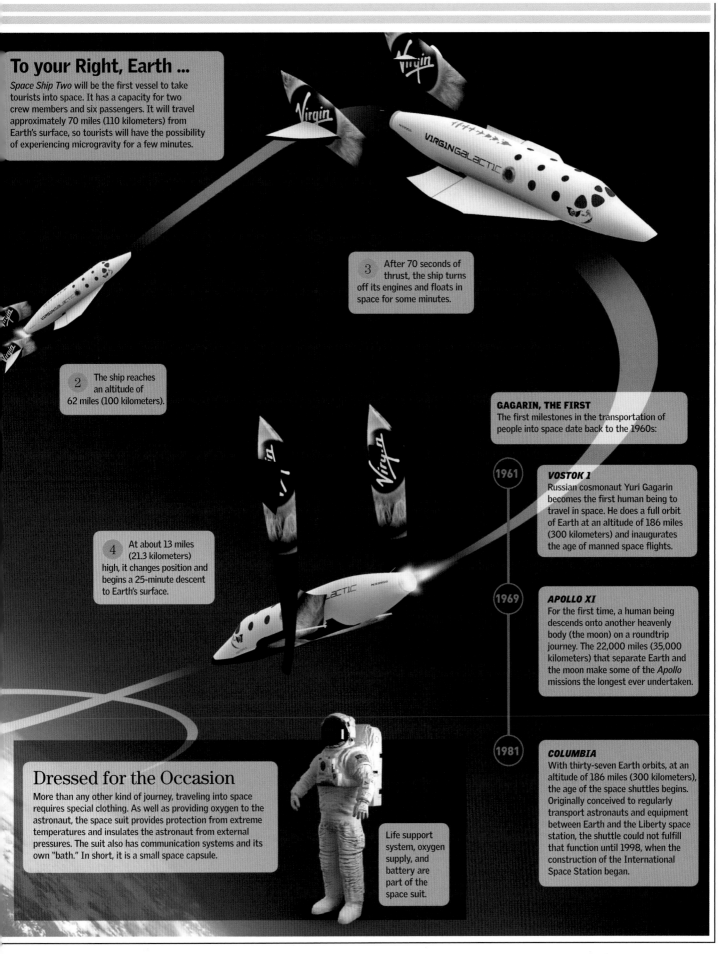

To your Right, Earth ...

Space Ship Two will be the first vessel to take tourists into space. It has a capacity for two crew members and six passengers. It will travel approximately 70 miles (110 kilometers) from Earth's surface, so tourists will have the possibility of experiencing microgravity for a few minutes.

3 After 70 seconds of thrust, the ship turns off its engines and floats in space for some minutes.

2 The ship reaches an altitude of 62 miles (100 kilometers).

GAGARIN, THE FIRST
The first milestones in the transportation of people into space date back to the 1960s:

1961

VOSTOK 1
Russian cosmonaut Yuri Gagarin becomes the first human being to travel in space. He does a full orbit of Earth at an altitude of 186 miles (300 kilometers) and inaugurates the age of manned space flights.

4 At about 13 miles (21.3 kilometers) high, it changes position and begins a 25-minute descent to Earth's surface.

1969

APOLLO XI
For the first time, a human being descends onto another heavenly body (the moon) on a roundtrip journey. The 22,000 miles (35,000 kilometers) that separate Earth and the moon make some of the *Apollo* missions the longest ever undertaken.

1981

COLUMBIA
With thirty-seven Earth orbits, at an altitude of 186 miles (300 kilometers), the age of the space shuttles begins. Originally conceived to regularly transport astronauts and equipment between Earth and the Liberty space station, the shuttle could not fulfill that function until 1998, when the construction of the International Space Station began.

Dressed for the Occasion

More than any other kind of journey, traveling into space requires special clothing. As well as providing oxygen to the astronaut, the space suit provides protection from extreme temperatures and insulates the astronaut from external pressures. The suit also has communication systems and its own "bath." In short, it is a small space capsule.

Life support system, oxygen supply, and battery are part of the space suit.

Working in Space

The profession of astronaut emerged as a result of the space expertise developed by the United States and the Soviet Union in the mid-twentieth century. Initially, it was only military pilots with specific technical knowledge who could travel in space. Later, these requirements disappeared, but the training remained extremely rigorous. To accustom themselves to life in space, astronauts exercise in zero-gravity conditions, spend hundreds of hours in flight simulators, work on IT programs, and adapt to difficult movements in reduced spaces.

Heroic Crews

The astronauts' theoretical training program includes astronomy, navigation, IT, meteorology, medicine, and physics. However, the physical training is the toughest obstacle. Initially, the astronauts prepare in airplanes with their interiors appropriately modified to artificially recreate the absence of gravity for periods of half a minute. During these moments of zero gravity, they must perform various activities, such as handling equipment, eating, and drinking. For more prolonged exercises under simulated conditions of weightlessness, specially conditioned swimming pools are used. People who are cut out for traveling in space do not tend to have illnesses, nor do they have claustrophobia. During the days before the launch, they are isolated to safeguard them against any contagious disease. For astronauts, the hours following the launch are the most difficult, because they are subject to dizziness and acute sensations of disorientation.

COMMUNICATION
Seeking to improve contact with satellites in orbit.

The Lunar Mission 2020

NASA plans to establish an outpost on the lunar surface to serve as a base for exploring Mars.

EXPLORATION
Robots controlled by astronauts.

1965
The first space walk took place during NASA's Project Gemini missions.

THE EVOLUTION OF ASTRONOMY

For millennia, human beings have analyzed outer space by observation from Earth. However, since the mid-twentieth century, it was possible to begin to explore it by sending up a number of satellites and manned missions, which became increasingly far-reaching.

1957
FIRST SATELLITE

Sputnik (left), the first artificial satellite in history, is launched into space by the Soviets. *Sputnik 2* is sent into orbit with Laika, a dog, as its crew.

1961
YURI GAGARIN

Yuri Gagarin (left) is the first human being in outer space onboard the Russian spaceship *Vostok I*. His journey lasts 108 minutes and he completes an orbit of Earth.

Routine Far from Home

Life in space may cause harmful effects on a number of biological systems. For this reason, specialists supervise the everyday activities of astronauts, imposing specific routines on them for every hour of the day. Physical exercises are fundamental, because the absence of gravity causes the loss of musculature.

1 **WORKING**
There is a work schedule onboard ship.

2 **EATING**
Regular hydration is essential.

3 **WASHING**
They shower every three days.

4 **SLEEPING**
They tie themselves down so that they do not float.

5 **EXERCISING**
They attempt to tone their muscles.

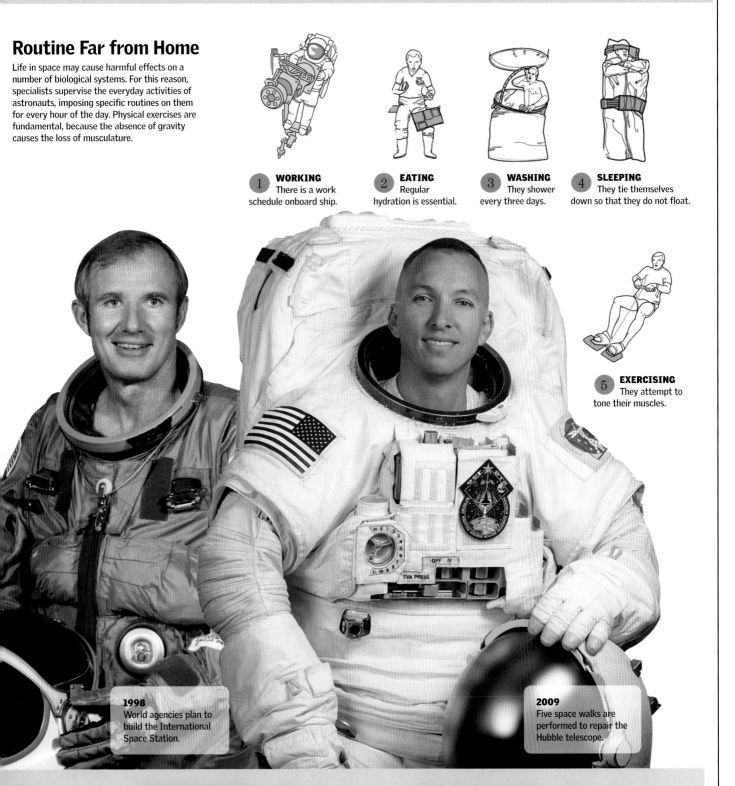

1998
World agencies plan to build the International Space Station.

2009
Five space walks are performed to repair the Hubble telescope.

1969
APOLLO XI

The first mission to land on the moon. Neil Armstrong (seated left, right) descends from the space module and takes a memorable walk on the moon's surface.

1984
DISCOVERY

The third shuttle orbiter (right), used to carry out various missions of research, observation, and assembly of the International Space Station, begins making its flights.

2009
FIXING THE HUBBLE

In a risky mission, the astronauts succeed in repairing the Hubble telescope and installing two new cameras—another landmark in the history of space exploration.

INDEX